Inside Leg, Outside Rein

by

Karen A. Stansbury

Lakeland Terrier Press, LLC

Lakeland Terrier Press, LLC
P.O. Box 181
Washington Depot, CT 06794

Cover cartoon by Dave May, Custom Cartoon Art
Cover design/layout by Deb Tremper, Six Penny Graphics
Logo design by Kelli Mincey, Cre8tive Mind Designs

Printed in the United States of America

Inside Leg, Outside Rein is a work of fiction. Names, characters, places, and incidents either are the product of the author's imagination, or are used fictitiously. Any resemblance to actual persons, living or dead, events or locales is entirely coincidental.

Also by Karen A. Stansbury

Eyes Up, Heels Down

Stay Balanced!

CONTENTS

Those who give up essential liberty, to preserve a little temporary safety, deserve neither liberty nor safety.

BENJAMIN FRANKLIN

I long to hear that you have declared an independency—and by the way in the new Code of Laws which I suppose it will be necessary for you to make I desire you would Remember the Ladies, and be more generous and favourable to them than your ancestors. Do not put such unlimited power into the hands of the Husbands. Remember all Men would be tyrants if they could.

ABIGAIL ADAMS TO JOHN ADAMS
MARCH 31, 1776

Dedicated to Tatum Bass

For Bravery

CHAPTER ONE

Washington's Spies

I t's been said that one should sit tight for one year after a divorce. Do not buy a house, the pundits counsel. Refrain from making any life changing decisions. Let the mourning process run its course.

I've never been particularly receptive to unsolicited advice.

"Where do we go first?" Carlie demanded. "There are about a million tables here!"

We were standing on the beautifully kept green of Tallmadge Academy for Girls in historic Bridge Hollow, located in Litchfield County, Connecticut. Across the Hunterbury River, Bridge Hollow School for Boys was also conducting Orientation Day for new students and their parents.

"There's the Registration table," I pointed. "Seems like the place to start."

Carlie Graham was my new Mentee. A scholarship student, and a sophomore transfer from her home town high school in northern Vermont, Carlie would be facing enormous academic and social challenges at Tallmadge Academy. The administration had asked me to step in as Carlie's local guide, philosopher and friend.

"Queen Bees at twelve o'clock," Carlie hissed, grabbing my arm.

New student packets were being distributed by two women in designer country wear. Their name tags designated them as TA alums, aged about forty summers. They each wore their light brown hair in a shoulder length up flip, which they tossed regularly.

I introduced Carlie.

"Oh yes," Exhibit A on the left drawled. "You're the new transfer girl." She attempted to wrinkle her frozen forehead. "From Maine, wasn't it?"

"Rural Vermont," Carlie replied. "My parents own a dairy farm, and can't get away much." She paused and smiled. "All that manure to shovel every day."

Impressive. My already favorable opinion of Carlie rose even higher.

"You'll be living in Kilbourne Hall," Exhibit B on the right informed her. She pointed her French manicured forefinger to a large stone building at one corner of the quadrangle. "It's the oldest dormitory on campus. Fireplaces in every room, huge windows. I lived there my junior year."

"Sounds a little chilly," I remarked, as Carlie and I moved along to the Activities and Sports area.

"Yeah, well. It's a lot colder up in the sticks."

The Tallmadge Academy Rowing Team was set up at the bottom of the green, near the bridge. The new boathouse, shared by both schools, was situated across the river. Coordinating banners of cherry red and gray, the TA colors, and navy blue and gray for BHS were hanging from the upper windows of the building. As part of their team display, the girls had brought over several pairs of long oars with blades painted in the school colors, and a double shell, which was perched on slings behind the team table.

Carlie, who had been rowing in the Lake Champlain area since she was eleven, had already won a place on the TA team. She was slated for the heavyweight eight, position to be determined.

Several of the alumni dads and grandads were hovering around the table, some wearing ancient blazers in navy and grey, with crossed oars on the breast pocket. Rowing in Bridge Hollow was clearly a generational sport.

The team captain, name of Therese Ellis, a large beefy blond in her final year at TA, waved to Carlie.

"There you are Graham!" She bellowed. "Glad to hear you'll be in the eight with us. Coach Curtis says you're going to be a terrific asset to the team. Well done!"

"Capital!" one of the grandfathers responded. "We'll look to you to help us win the Championship, young lady." He turned to one of the fathers, also be-jacketed, who nodded emphatically.

"We can't allow Holmes Academy to carry off the trophy again this year," the younger man added. "I've been speaking to the Coach about better and longer drills for practice this season."

"Oh good." Carlie gave them a tight lipped grimace. "This is Emma Carbury, my new Mentor. She rows too."

"Aha," exclaimed yet another dad. "Then you must come out for Masters rowing with us. Five a.m., four mornings a week! Six o'clock on Saturdays. We like to sleep in on the weekends."

There was a hearty sporting chuckle from the herd. I could feel my knees buckle.

"Emma's a new adjunct member of the teaching staff," Carlie the Helpful continued. "And she's a trial lawyer."

"Excellent!" Grandad number one replied. "I'll alert the Coach directly."

"You know," I whispered fiercely to my teenaged charge, as we moved toward the refreshment table, "If I wanted to be abused like this, I'd go have lunch with my mother."

She looked at me in obvious surprise. "What? One of those guys may be single. You've got to get out there at *some* point Emma. I've seen you in black Lycra. Come on! You're hot, independent, and eligible. Time to work it."

A small boned female in a peach pantsuit walked to the center of the green with a bull horn.

"Would all new students and their parents kindly begin moving toward the chapel? The program will begin in fifteen minutes."

The chapel had been built in 1799 in the classic cruciform design, with white box pews and huge plain glass windows. The Headmistress of Tallmadge Academy for Girls, Yolanda Gibbs, stood at the lectern.

"Good morning, and welcome to one of the oldest schools for young women in the United States. Founded in 1798 by several graduates of nearby Litchfield Female Academy, Tallmadge is named for Litchfield's famous resident, Major Benjamin Tallmadge. A valued officer of General Washington during the Revolutionary War, the major settled in the town of Litchfield in 1784, was elected to Congress in 1801, and enjoyed many years of prosperity until his death in 1835.

"Other famous Litchfield residents include Ethan Allen of the Green Mountain Boys, Aaron Burr, and Oliver Wolcott, who served as a delegate to the Continental Congress, was one of the signers of the Declaration of Independence, and was appointed to command a regiment of Connecticut militia. And for all of the lawyers in the audience, the first law school in the United States was opened by Judge Tapping Reeve at the end of the Revolution, and still stands on South Street in Litchfield, around the corner from the courthouse.

"What most people don't know is that Major Tallmadge of the

Second Connecticut Light Dragoons was also Chief of Intelligence under General Washington. The members of the Culper Ring, so called for Washington's land in Culpeper County, Virginia, were America's first spies.

"The Culpers were organized by Tallmadge and operated from 1778 until the end of the War of Independence. Their mission was to keep General Washington informed about the activities of the British. At the time the British forces were occupying New York City, and the Culper operatives used various methods to transmit information across the Long Island Sound to Tallmadge's headquarters in Fairfield, Connecticut. These tools included double agents, code books, invisible ink, dead drops, spreading disinformation, and even signals via laundry lines. Secrecy was so imperative that the General himself did not know the true identities of all of his spies.

"A few personal items regarding Tallmadge. First, Nathan Hale had been a close friend of Benjamin Tallmadge's at Yale, and the tragedy of Hale's capture and subsequent hanging by the British in New York was no doubt one of the reasons that General Washington was diligent in support of his Intelligence Service. Second, it was Major Tallmadge who discovered that Benedict Arnold had committed treason. Had his suspicions been acted upon, Arnold never would have escaped to England.

"In those days, we must remember, Americans had considered themselves British subjects until the signing of the Declaration of Independence on July fourth, 1776. Therefore, even after the War began, it was often impossible to discern Patriot from Tory. Everyone spoke the same language. Loyalties were blurred and uncertain.

"Several major trade routes ran straight through Litchfield, and here in the Lake Washington area, so named for our revered General and first President. Due to the lack of navigable water, this region was considered safe from attack by the British, and therefore became an important depot for munitions and military supplies, which were then moved to strategic American posts in the Hudson River Valley. The town of Litchfield was the location of a prison for captured British soldiers, many of whom remained after the war was over, and raised families here.

"Due to the importance of communications and supply lines, patriot residents in this part of Connecticut were ever on the alert for signs of betrayal by their neighbors. The communities around Lake Washington, positioned equidistant between Litchfield and the New York State line, included various Tory spies amongst their American denizens."

Headmistress Gibbs paused, and smiled graciously at her audience. "Which brings me, finally, to our affiliate across the Hunterbury River. Bridge Hollow School for Boys. At the time of the Revolution, that is to say, 1775 until 1783, our Tallmadge Academy property was pasture land for grazing cattle. As the bend in the river created an easy access to the lake, the town of Bridge Hollow existed on the opposite bank, and the school was built in 1771 to prepare the sons of wealthy residents for the law, or the church. Girls were, for the most part, taught at home by their mothers. It was deemed that book learning was not nearly as important to a woman's education as her instruction in the domestic arts."

"Housework," Carlie whispered.

"Abigail Adams," Gibbs continued, "wife of our second President, once wrote that she was never sent to any school, and that female education in the best of families was limited to writing and arithmetic, with some rare instances of music and dancing.

"In the eighteenth century, boys entered BHS at about twelve years of age, and lived there until they were ready for college. Their curriculum included English history, various mathematics, Latin, philosophy, astronomy and geography. Books and paper were scarce in those days, and candlelight was the only illumination after the sun went down.

"The Headmaster at the time the school opened was a man named Joshua Morrison. Like Tapping Reeve, Morrison was a judge turned schoolmaster. He and his wife Hannah lived at BHS from 1771 until early 1780, when the couple left the area suddenly. Although there were numerous rumors regarding their disappearance, no documentation has ever been found. One of the stories included witchcraft. Hannah was known to practice the Old Religion, and she often provided herbs and potions for the locals.

"Today the town of Bridge Hollow spans each side of the river, and students cross the Woodruff foot bridge many times in a day to take classes and attend events at both schools. The dormitory monitors are careful, however, to ascertain that boys and girls are in their appropriate bedrooms at night." Laughter. "I will now turn over the podium to our Deputy Headmistress, Laurel Collier, who will introduce our full time staff, and share our goals for the academic year."

"So what do you think?" I asked Carlie, as we moved with the masses back out on to the green. "Feeling comfortable about your decision to come here?"

"So far, so good, I guess," she replied, scanning the crowd. Sitting alone on a bench near the library was a woman, and a girl about Carlie's age. Their isolation from the rest of the throng was obvious. Carlie took my elbow and immediately began walking in their direction.

"Do you mind if we join you?" I asked.

"I just transferred here as a sophomore," Carlie added, introducing herself, "so I want to get to know people."

"I'm Sophie Sullivan," the woman replied. "And this is my daughter, Julie. Julie is also a transfer second year, and I believe that you two are on the same floor in Kilbourne. I just saw your name on the roster."

"Have you checked out your room yet?" Julie asked Carlie.

"No, we were just heading there now. Want to go together?"

The third floor of Kilbourne Hall was teeming with students and parents, scurrying up and down the hall with suitcases, laundry baskets and various other necessaries of dorm life. We located Julie's new home first, number seventeen. The large windows had a nice view of the quad, and she and her roommates would have a strategic advantage with morning showers. Each suite on this floor had a good size common room with working fireplace and wall telephone, a powder room, and two bedrooms, each set up with two single beds, two desks with built in bookcases, and two bedside tables with lamps. "Closets!" Carlie cried, opening one. "Lots of space, and shelves. Thank goodness. I hope they're all like this," she added.

"When are you moving in?" I asked Julie.

"We're local," Sophie explained, "so I thought we'd come tomorrow morning, when the chaos has subsided a bit. Better parking then."

"We'll do the same. Carlie's been staying with me for the past week. I'm local too," I added, "but new to the area. We're part of TA's new Mentor/Mentee program for out of state students."

"I read about that in the school paper. I thought it was a wonderful idea. High school children shouldn't be so far away from home without a support system."

Sophie bent to check if one of the lamps had a bulb in it, and I noticed the bracelet on her left wrist. It was beautiful. Pink stones and sparkling crystal beads were alternated with pearls on a silver chain, at the end of which dangled a silver pentacle. A five pointed star enclosed in a circle. The symbol for Wicca.

"Are you a member of a coven, Sophie?" I asked, interested. "Or are you a sole practitioner?"

Sophie grinned. "Oh, I'm a solo. I don't do well in groups. Never have. Which are you?"

"Neither. Yet. I've been learning Shamanic healing for the past year or so. Lots of journeys and soul retrievals, a couple of webinars on animal communication. I even tried a drumming circle. Shamanism just isn't calling me. So I'm open to finding what does."

We were walking down the hall, toward the other end of the building. The girls had gone ahead to explore Carlie's suite.

"Witches never advertise. We don't believe in it, and the historical stigma is still so strong. But if you're interested, I have a suggestion," Sophie replied. "The local bookstore has an excellent selection of Wiccan research materials. I would recommend anything by Scott Cunningham, and don't be afraid to try *The Complete Idiot's Guide* series. They're surprisingly comprehensive. *Wicca and Witchcraft* first, and then perhaps *Spells and Spellcraft*. And by all means, visit me at my gardening store. It's called *Root and Branch* on Lakeview Road. I can address most of your gardening needs, especially if you like herbs. I also have a complete stock of supplies for practitioners of the Craft," she added quietly. "And I teach. Come and see."

"This is a high school level course on Evidence," I announced to the blur of young faces in front of me. "My name is Emma Carbury, and I've been practicing law in Connecticut's state and federal courts for nearly twenty years. Whether or not you are an aspiring attorney, the materials we cover this semester will be invaluable to you as you attend college and graduate school, and beyond.

"You will note at the top of your syllabus that I plan to cover such topics as hearsay, the credibility of witnesses, and expert opinions. We will be following Connecticut state law. Any questions so far?"

A large young man with dark hair raised his hand. "Do you give extra credit for additional assignments?"

"No." I replied, firmly. "But my exams are take home essays, so that ought to be a load off your minds."

They laughed.

"We will have a mid term and a final, which count for sixty percent of your grade. The remaining forty percent will be my assessment of your classroom participation. For those of you who believe that you are law school bound, this course will be a learning experience at another level. Most law professors give only a final exam, and if you are deemed unprepared for three classes, you are automatically dropped."

Murmurs of dismay. "But don't worry. That kind of grading is not permitted here, more's the pity."

Laughter again. These kids were easily amused.

"The textbook that I've had you buy is actually a hornbook, or treatise, for first year law students. We'll cherry pick what we need from it, and I will supplement the reading with handouts of magazine and newspaper articles. Occasionally I'll have you watch a television program, a movie, or review something pertinent on the Internet. Our goal this term is not to turn you into litigating sharks. I want you to leave this course in December with the ability to think for yourselves, and to analyze carefully what you have heard, seen, and read. For the rest of your lives, if we're lucky.

"Let's start with some background questions. If you believe everything you read, see, or hear in the media, please raise your hand."

Most of the class shot their arms up like rockets.

"OK! We have our work cut out for us. Another question. If someone posts a comment on a Facebook page, do you assume that what they are saying is fact?"

Every hand this time.

"What about photos? For example, if a snapshot of someone's big toe shows up on your cell phone, purporting to be part of Suzie's foot, does it logically follow that Suzie has recently dropped her sock, and has knowingly disseminated the results for your enjoyment?"

"Why shouldn't it?" A femme fatale in the front row demanded. "We know that the picture comes from Suzie because of caller ID."

"But what if Suzie has taken a picture of Megan's toe in the locker room, without Megan's knowledge?" I argued. "Or in the alternative, Megan grabbed Suzie's phone and clicked away, while poor Suzie was trying on bathing suits?"

More murmurs. Clearly this was new and exciting thinking for these children.

"So my question to you is this: How do you know? The Rules of Evidence were drafted for the federal court system, and each state, as a means of introducing probative information into the litigation process, thereby separating the wheat from the chaff."

"What about the stuff that teachers are telling us in class, every day?" A thin young woman with large glasses inquired. "We can't leap up and discredit them in front of everyone," she grinned. "Or can we?"

I grinned back. "Excellent question! This would be a great time to talk about boundaries of behavior. You are all juniors and seniors in this room, correct?"

General nods of assent.

"And you're all still minors? All right. I vaguely remember those days! You have no legal rights, and you are required to do what every adult you know tells you, or you'll get into trouble. CYA people! Cover your big toe. The point is, if the person in the front of the room wants you to believe that Leo Tolstoy was the greatest writer in the world, and that same person is giving you the grade that will be reviewed by college admissions committees, take that into account when you write your paper on *War and Peace*."

"So why bother learning these rules, if we can never say what we think?" Therese the rowing captain hollered, without raising her hand.

"First of all," I replied, using my best courtroom voice, "even as a minor you have a duty to yourself to speak up when your gut tells you that it's important. Second, once you're an adult, there will be plenty of people out there who should be hearing what you think, as long as you express yourself with civility. People like doctors, sales people, and contractors who are putting additions on your house. Third, I'm one of those people who *is* giving you a grade, and I like respect. Please raise your hand from now on in my classroom."

Ms. Ellis grumbled something to her neighbor, and they both laughed. My bully antennae became activated. I made a mental note to ask Carlie about her later.

"Today we are going to begin with the legal definition of hearsay. Please take a look at your handouts. We'll divide into groups and work on the example scenarios."

At three o'clock class ended, and I released my students to their various activities and sports practices. The powers that be had allotted us a conference room in the oldest wing of the Bridge Hollow School library. The large white clapboard building was an elegant example of pre Revolutionary architecture, with working fireplaces, wide plank floors, and enormous twelve over twelve pane windows. Walnut tables and study carrels lined the moss green walls, and the bookcases were arranged comfortably to create quiet reading areas on two floors. The only nod to the twenty-first century was the computer room, with the DVD collection and copy center beyond.

I needed to get back to my office across the bridge, but instead, wandered over to a window seat, kicked off my high heels, and arranged myself against a pillow, looking out toward the water. Rowers from both teams were carrying eights and fours down to the dock. I watched boat after boat pull away and move swiftly down the river toward the lake. The September sun was strong, and my day had started in Westport early that morning. My head fell back on to the pillow.

I am in the same room, but it is twilight, and the candles are lighted. Boys are seated at the numerous tables; the only sound is the turning of pages, or from time to time, the scratching of quills on paper. I walk slowly down the rows, a candlestick in my left hand. My skirt makes no sound on the wood floor as I patrol, alert for students who are wasting time, or disturbing the others. Most of the boys ignore me, but Christopher, seated a little apart from the rest as always, looks up and smiles. I allow my face to beam back to him, as I place my forefinger on my lips. I know that my husband is coming soon, and he can be severe with the horsewhip. I continue with my walking.

I woke up, still alone in the darkening room. I heard one of the librarians come in and flick on the overhead light switch. The rowers were maneuvering back to the docks after practice. I saw Carlie in her bright red team windbreaker, and reached down for my shoes.

CHAPTER TWO

Boundaries

Six months after celebrating the soothing balm of divorce, I had relocated an hour north from Southport, Connecticut to bucolic Litchfield County. I bought a small, gray shingled house with its own dock on Lake Washington, and spent the summer kayaking and swimming, while gutting the kitchen and the two and a half baths.

My law partner Denise Frederickson and I had devised a plan which entailed my driving back and forth to Westport as needed, on a flexible schedule. The remainder of the time I would work on building a satellite practice in Bridge Hollow. I had connected with a small firm that I knew by reputation, and the principals and I had agreed on an office share arrangement.

I had moved my beloved mare to Apple Ridge Farm, a large commercial barn just fifteen minutes from my house. Joy had all day turnout with two male buddies, and our new trainer, Joanne, experienced in both jumping and dressage, was teaching us lateral movement. Our goals were to build Joy's top line muscles, improve her trot and canter transitions, and get her more responsive to my leg. Joanne had a quiet, compassionate manner of teaching, and thus far, appeared to be free of any major psychological issues.

The Bridge Hollow News had run a story about my arrival in town, complete with a crowd pleasing shot of my Lakeland Terrier, Abby and me, standing by the gazebo on the town green. The journalist had highlighted my work with CAPW, the professional women's networking group that Denise and I co-chaired, and the articles that I had written and posted on the website for public perusal. One article, *Why Every High School Student Should Learn the Rules of Evidence: A basic understanding of hearsay, credibility, and expert opinions,* drew some attention. The Heads of Bridge Hollow School and Tallmadge Academy had jointly requested that I teach a class on Evidence at the prep school level. I had agreed to try it for a semester.

Once I'd signed a teaching contract, I was suddenly thrust into the new Mentor program, and Carlie Graham had strolled into my life.

At fifteen Carlie had the confidence and self possession that most adults three times her age were still striving to achieve. Slightly shorter than my five foot nine, Carlie had long dark blond hair, hazel eyes, and a powerful athletic build from years of farm work and rowing. She was also a natural scholar. For Carlie, learning was an adventure. We had connected as close friends almost immediately.

Carlie had requested a weekend at my house, and a break from the dorm. Saturday morning we discussed our agenda for the day.

I talked her into letting me pay for manicures and pedicures.

"I've never done this before, Emma," Carlie said. "I'm not sure how I'm going to react to some stranger touching my feet."

"Just give into it. I used to think that women who pampered themselves were spoiled. But now I get it. You're going to spend most of your life surrounded by people who expect you to take care of them. Spa visits are total luxuries that you can indulge in, just for yourself. Don't feel weird about it."

"OK. But I'm pretty ticklish."

An hour later, we left the salon, hands and toes in matching pearly pink.

"What's your pleasure for the rest of day?" I asked her. "Besides the inevitable stop at the bookstore?"

"Can I think about it while I eat?"

"Yes, of course. If you don't mind, I have to make a quick visit to the tack shop before we get lunch. I promise to be speedy."

"This place is amazing!" Carlie said, exhibiting new energy. "It's like a fancy mall for horse people!"

I left her to wander around the store, while I sat on the floor and pulled out leather ankle boots from the shelf, looking for a pair of size threes. Lindsay hurried over to help me.

"Your mare has to have fleece lined?"

"Unfortunately. The plain leather gives her terrible rubs."

"Here we are. What else do you need?"

"Another canister of those molasses treats that Joy likes."

"They're over by the register now."

As sole suppliers for the Tallmadge Academy riding team, Bridge Hollow Tack stocked everything that was horsey, from blankets, saddles, and bridles to gifts and treats. They had a tailor and a saddler on staff.

"I heard that Frank Shaw is training at your barn now," Lindsay remarked, handing back my debit card.

"That he is," I replied.

"What do you think of him?"

Tack shop employees were usually human banks of information.

"I think he's an arrogant jackass, but that opinion is based on only about ten minutes of association."

"Always go with first impressions," Lindsay said. "Frank was at

Mel Ramsey's barn for a few years. He has a reputation for being a rider, not a horseman."

"Do you know why he changed farms?"

"No," Lindsay responded, thoughtfully. "But now I'm going to find out."

Carlie and I consumed tuna melts in the Bostwick Tavern pub. As we finished up, I decided on a sneak tactic. "Let's stop at Parfumerie Micheline. I'm low on moisturizer."

We moved past the shelves of designer body lotions and approached the Chanel counter. A stunning brunette in a black smock was making up a young blond woman. Carlie paused, fascinated. The Chanel consultant looked over at us and smiled. "I am almost finished here," she said with a charming French accent. "Would either of you care to be next?"

"My friend would love to be next," I replied, and steered Carlie over to the other stool.

"Did you know that they were doing makeovers here today, Emma?" Carlie looked suspicious.

"*Naturellement*," I replied. "You're going to love it."

"What marvelous skin!" The French woman remarked. "*Je m'appelle Claudine.* And you are called?"

"Carlie. Uh, Carlotta."

"You are very pretty, Carlotta. You pluck the eyebrows, yes?"

"Yes."

"*Alors.* Let us start with some mascara. *Bleu, ou violet, peut-être?*"

"Blue would be great, thanks."

I browsed in the perfumes. I put a jar of Chanel No. 5 body powder into my basket, and moved over to the moisturizers. By the time I was finished checking out, Carlie had been transformed into an elegant young woman.

"I have used our new bronzer," Claudine explained, "and the

palest pink over the eyes, and on the lips. Carlotta does not require much makeup. This is violet on the lower lashes, for her to make the comparison."

"What do you think Carlie?"

"I look like I'm in college!" She exclaimed, staring at herself in the mirror.

"We'll take one of everything that you've applied, then please," I said. "Plus some of the violet mascara and the bronzer for me, as well. And we're both entitled to some new brushes."

Carlie looked horrified. "That's going to be a lot, isn't it?" She whispered. "I don't want Mom to be upset...."

"Don't worry, I'll talk to your mom. I think a trip to the café is in order, now. Don't you?"

We stood in line at Bridge Hollow's Coffee Common, a hot spot for students from both schools. A few of Carlie's contemporaries were in evidence, talking in groups, or sitting alone at round tables with their laptops.

"Oh no!" I cried, pointing to a corner by the window. A huge flat panel screen was silently displaying one of the cable news channels. "Not this place too!"

Carlie smirked. "What's your problem?"

I turned to her. "Please explain to me the modern obsession with electronic connection. If folks aren't texting or emailing, they're glued to some form of digital screen in a semi comatose state, reading incomprehensible comments from thousands of strangers, or being bombarded with more information than most computers could handle."

"Yeah. So?"

"What's the fascination? It seems more like an addiction than anything else. How does anyone ever get to sleep?"

Carlie shrugged. "People just like to know what's going on."

I gave up. "I don't even have cable at home. Let's go outside with our drinks."

We took our ice lattes across the street and sat on one of the benches by the Hunterbury River. To the north we could just make out the Woodruff foot bridge, and the beautiful open fields with hills beyond. The two historic boarding schools, Tallmadge Academy for Girls, on our bank of the river, and Bridge Hollow School for Boys, faced each other from either side of the water. The boathouse, on the BHS bank, was a hive of activity.

We sat in silence for a few minutes. Carlie was staring sadly at the screen of her cell phone. A snapshot of a young man was waving back at her.

I had learned that direct questions were the recommended form of communication with Carlie.

"Your mom said in her latest email that you had a pretty rough freshman year. Was it school work, or crew, or something else?"

"It wasn't school," Carlie mumbled, her straw in her mouth.

"Was it a boy?"

She looked up. "How did you know?"

"I remember high school, Carlotta. Homecoming games, dances, parties that became make out sessions until someone's parent sent us home. Parking. Raging hormones."

"His name is Kirk," Carlie said. "He was in my sister Jackie's class."

"Wow, so a senior. Is he going to college this fall?"

"Yes, to Brown." She seemed to deflate as she spoke.

"What's wrong Carlie?"

"Well, Kirk was very popular in school. Straight A's, AP classes, co-captain of the football and track teams, Student Government. We weren't able to spend a lot of time together."

"Are you still officially dating this guy?"

"I've tried to break up twice, but he got so upset, I just let it go."

"Why do you want to break up?"

Carlie finished her drink. "It just seemed like it was time. He's in Rhode Island. I'm here. I know it's an easier distance than Vermont would have been, but I thought I was doing the right thing."

"New schools, new lives, new people?"

"Something like that. Yeah."

"Did he take you to his Senior Prom?"

"Yes. It's so different with his friends. They aren't kids that I would normally hang out with. Too old, for one thing. And they like to party. Most of them are on the football team. I'm kind of quiet, you know? I like to be home, reading or watching movies. I don't think that making lots of noise and breaking rules is fun."

"Your parents should erect a statue to you," I said drily.

"I get why a grown up would see it that way," she continued, "but Kirk took a lot of ribbing from them about me. I'm not a cheerleader or anything. And I sure didn't put out."

That answered that question.

"Well, gold star to Kirk, then, don't you think? Because he doesn't respond to peer pressure?"

"I guess."

"Does he say why he doesn't want to stop going out with you?"

"He says he loves me. He says that he feels at home with me, that I relax him. He doesn't have to impress me like he does everyone else. Especially his parents."

"Do you feel that way about him?"

"I feel at home when I'm *at* home. With my family."

"It sounds as though you're more of a comfortable couch than a girlfriend. Sorry, that's a little strong."

Carlie looked interested. "No, you're right."

"I think women prefer, in general, to be told how exciting they are. I'd like to know that I keep a man awake, not put him to sleep."

"Exactly!"

"Here's a little secret that all married women know, Carlie. Men, with a few special exceptions, want their significant others to provide for them all the mothering that they never got from their actual mothers. They will not express this out loud, but it is implicit. The key is to know when you've crossed the boundary from main squeeze to nanny. I'm not saying that there are clear signs, either."

"Giving him a back rub after a football game?"

"That's probably OK."

"Helping him do laundry?"

"Borderline. Depends where you are in the relationship."

"How about wrapping all the gifts he got his family for Christmas?"

"Definitely smacks of Mary Poppins. What does this guy actually *do for you?*"

"He came over for dinner every Sunday night. Sometimes he helped me with my math homework."

"Sorry, darling, but I agree with you that it's time to cut bait. Kirk sounds like an energy drain." I paused. "Want to hear my theory of Dump and Suck?"

Carlie grinned. "Shoot."

"Whenever you hook up with anyone, romantically or otherwise, ask yourself the following question: Do I feel energized, or depleted, when I'm with this person? If the answer is the latter, then this person is probably guilty of Dump and Suck. In essence, he or she has dumped their emotional baggage on you, and then sucked all the good stuff out of you. You are left feeling like the limp noodles at the bottom of a Chinese take out container."

"That's it!" Carlie laughed. "Day old chicken lo mein!" She thought for a moment. "But I'm not good at telling people how I really feel. It's easier to be, well, you know."

"A sassy smart mouth? Ha! I was the same way. When my sister and I were your age," I began, conscious of the *Father Knows Best* moment, "our mother would treat us to a daily harping on the status of having boyfriends. Kate and I were brainwashed into believing that *any* man, no matter how unsuitable, was better than no man at all. It's probably why I settled and married Shawn the Lemon right out of law school. The point is, had Audrey trained us to be more discerning, more aware of how much we deserved from a relationship, I never would have even *dated* Shawn, much less married him. But, that's Audrey. A woman who is still following rules that someone, she knows not whom, made up circa 1875."

"So you think that my family has taught me that dating is better than being alone?"

"I think that somehow *you* have convinced yourself that being part of a couple is better than being single. Do you honestly believe that, sitting here?"

"No. Jackie never has boyfriends, and it doesn't seem to bother her."

"Well, good for Jackie, but we're talking about you. Do you realize how terrific you are?"

"I know that I'm a super brain, because everyone says so. And I'm a good athlete."

"That's a start. But when you understand your value as a person, all will become clear. It's the secret to everything. Once you begin to demand boundaries in relationships, and you decide how you deserve to be treated, none of this will ever happen to you again. Or, at least, not for very long. Do you understand?"

"I think I do. Thanks."

"Good. Now, I thought we'd go to Portobello's for dinner tonight. Their gnocchi is unbelievable. Do you like pesto sauce?"

Carlie had requested the big guest room, which had a view of the lake from two windows. I had made up the bed in pretty hydrangea sheets, and put a vase of yellow and white roses on her bookcase.

"Now, recall the Terrier Caveat," I said. "Terriers are inclined to evil, so don't leave anything within Abby's range, if you ever want to see it again. Especially previously worn under garments. They are particular terrier delicacies."

"Got it. What's the dress code for tonight?"

"Nice casual."

"Great. I'll try my new make up."

We were seated next to a big group, which was made up of three couples and, alas, their three new babies. I ordered a glass of chardonnay. One of the fathers was swinging his progeny up and down, while emitting a strange eh, eh, eh noise.

Conversation became difficult. I was considering making a request for a change of venue when a man in a double breasted striped suit, two tables in the other direction, got up and headed straight for us.

"Incoming," I mouthed to Carlie.

The man advanced to my chair and gave me one of those heavy, hearty slaps on the back that usually sends the recipient face first into her appetizer.

"Emma! I was gonna call you next week! We gotta problem with the new restaurant."

"I'm sorry to hear that, Mario. This is my friend Carlotta."

"Nice to meetcha. What do you say, Emma? You wanna talk about this now, over at my table?"

"No, I think Monday morning at the office will be just fine. Why don't you call me?"

"Will do! Hey, Susannah, get me another chianti!" The waitress made an expressive hand gesture. Mario relieved us of his presence.

"Does he come here a lot?" Carlie asked.

"He's the owner," I replied. "And a new client. He's starting another business on Candlewood Lake, near the marina. I guess he's having some trouble with the town."

"Can't imagine why," Carlie replied, sarcastically. "He could use one of your lectures on boundaries in relationships."

When the waiter came back to take our dessert orders, he informed us that after dinner drinks were on the house. We looked over at Mario, who beamed and waved. We requested two decaf cappuccinos.

As we left the restaurant twenty minutes later, the parents were passing the babies back and forth across the table, like damp bread baskets.

Abigail was not in her usual greet-us-at-the-door position.

She was, in fact, in the library, reclined on my tartan club chair, and busily mutilating something blue.

"OH NO!" Carlie shrieked. "My new bra!" She lunged for Abby.

With tail wagging, and delicate cotton lace hanging out from one side of her canine grin, Abby hopped off the chair and bounded through to the kitchen. A five minute game of catch the terrier ensued. In the end, we resorted to bribery. "TREATS!" I bellowed. Abs immediately dropped her prize and parked by the fridge, a picture of innocence.

Carlie dangled her lingerie by one finger. It was shredded and slimy. There was no hope of recovery. "I was so careful about my room," she said mournfully, "and then I left this by the sink in the bathroom."

"And thus, you were terrier-ized. I'm so sorry. We'll go to town tomorrow and get you something to replace it."

CHAPTER THREE

Innocence

My Book Club traveled north on Saturday morning to view my newly remodeled lake house, and to discuss Edith Wharton's Pulitzer Prize winning masterpiece *The Age of Innocence*.

"Tour please!" Eliot directed, handing me a bottle of chardonnay. "I've been hearing about this place all summer. Whoa! Nice kitchen!" She opened the wine refrigerator and surveyed the various labels.

"I like to cook," I replied, "and it's a hell of a lot more fun in your own place, just the way you want it, making meals for people you enjoy."

"You went with the verdigris color for the cabinets," Dottie mused, running her hand across the white granite top of the island. "I like it. Feels airy and clean."

Denise beckoned the ladies to the library. "This is my favorite room in the house," she sighed. I had knocked out the wall that separated the small living and dining rooms, and had created a big reading room which faced the back porch. A line of white French doors opened out on to surround views of the lake. There were two round tables with chairs, assorted groupings of club chairs and sofas in blues and greens, window seats, my cherry wood desk in one corner, and a wood burning fireplace. Built in book shelves lined the two side walls, and both sides of the fire. There were candlesticks on every table.

"It's like the Gryffindor common room!" Dottie exclaimed. "Just not circular."

"And no giant squid in the lake. Come upstairs."

There were two good sized guest rooms with a full bath between them, and a large master bedroom with a connected bath.

"Carlie is living in the dorm now, so her room is available," I explained, showing them through the door across the hall from mine, with its queen size bed and blue and yellow color scheme. "There's also this room, with two twins, so I can accommodate most, if not all of you, in case we get carried away with the margaritas this afternoon. My next project will be to finish the basement. I've always wanted a real artist's studio."

We looked at my bedroom last. There was a moment of silence.

"What?" I asked, a little nervous. "You saw most of this furniture in the Southport house."

"Yeah, but not with a balcony on the lake, and a fireplace," Eliot grinned. "This house is heaven," she breathed.

"Small, but heavenly," I agreed.

"Not small, Em," Angela said gently. "Cozy. It's a happy house. The colors are perfect. There's even a little pink in this room. The candles on your dressing table, the throw on your chaise. You've disdained girl shades for most of your life. Complained they were too feminine. This is quite a change."

"Maybe I'm softening a bit."

"All you need now is a real man," Dottie remarked, opening the French doors and walking outside. "This view is amazing," she said. "I can see the school teams practicing on the lake."

"Carlie's out there somewhere," I said, joining her.

"You're really enjoying this fake mommy thing, aren't you?" Denise asked.

"Well, it's nice when they're self sufficient and only come home on weekends. Much less work," I replied. "And no legal responsibility. Carlie's a great kid. Smart, funny, says what she thinks. But compassionate and thoughtful too. A perfect Mentee, really."

Half an hour later we were assembled on the porch with food and ice tea.

"Edith Wharton. Who wants to go first?" Angela asked.

Denise picked up her copy of *The Age of Innocence*. "She was born Edith Newbold Jones in 1862, into one of the last leisured class families of Old New York. This was a rigidly controlled society that discouraged women from any occupation other than marriage and motherhood. Supposedly the saying 'Keeping up with the Joneses' refers to Edith's father's family.

"Wharton was educated at home, and went on to write over forty books in forty years. She had an insider's experience of the privileged classes, and utilizing dramatic irony and subtle satire, wrote insightful psychological exposés of the period. Her main theme was the condition of women in society—the issues of infidelity, illegitimacy, and the repression and misery of the marriage tie. Along with her Pulitzer Prize, Wharton was the first woman to be awarded an honorary Doctorate of Letters from Yale University, and a full membership to the American Academy of Arts and Letters."

Denise checked her notes. "She married Edward, known as Teddy, Wharton in 1885, and for the next several years they spent their time amongst the high society of Newport, Rhode Island, and in Europe. Edith Wharton designed and built her estate 'The Mount' in Lenox, Massachusetts in 1902. She believed that the decoration of a home, and the composition of gardens, should honor the principles of harmony, simplicity, and proportion. She co-authored *The Decoration of Houses* with Ogden Codman in 1897.

"In 1903 Wharton became close friends with novelist Henry James, until his death in 1916. James was a profound influence on her writing. Wharton's marriage was not happy. Teddy suffered from mental illness, and embezzled money from her trust fund, of which he was a trustee, to support his mistress. Edith had a three year affair with an American journalist, one Morton Fullerton, moved to France permanently, and finally divorced Teddy in 1913. She received several prestigious awards for her charitable efforts toward refugees during World War I, and was buried in the American Cemetery at Versailles in 1937."

"What a woman!" Eliot exclaimed.

"*The Age of Innocence* was finished in Provence in 1920, and she won the Pulitzer for literature in 1921. Additionally, Wharton was the author of at least eighty-five short stories, and was particularly well regarded for the ones that featured ghosts." Denise concluded.

"Excellent Denise," Angela said. "Plot summary?"

"Newland Archer is a young lawyer who lives in New York, meaning Manhattan, of the 1870s, with his mother and spinster sister," Eliot began. "Their family is of the old guard, as Wharton's was. As the saga opens, Newland is about to become engaged to May Welland, also a member of one of the good old families. But there is a glitch. May's cousin Ellen, now the scandalous Countess Olenska, has returned to New York to escape her creepy Count husband, who is still in Europe. Newland announces his engagement quickly to show support for May's family, only to find himself falling in love with the free thinking Countess. The rest of the novel concerns Newland's struggle between his iron clad ties to the tribe, and his desperate desire to escape same."

Eliot paused. "What was so bad about the Count Olenski? Did anyone ever figure that out? Did he hit her? Was he into kinky stuff? Maybe the group thing? Animals? Or did he just plain cheat?"

"That's never made clear," Angela said. "Which is part of the problem, I guess. These people never spoke of anything distasteful, so problems were not addressed. They had an absolute talent for ignoring anything unpleasant. For all we know, the Count merely had the occasional fling with a maid. Ellen is determined never to return to her husband, and in fact does not, even though she is forced to give up her right to any of the marital property."

"Maybe he was verbally cruel to her," I added, thinking of my former marriage. "Bullying doesn't have to be physical, you know. Devaluing and isolation from the herd can be just as traumatizing, and much harder to prove, or understand. No visible evidence."

"OK, I get that," Eliot retorted. "So to make matters even worse, Ellen runs off with her husband's secretary?"

"Note that the Count was deemed within his rights to behave as atrociously as he chose," I remarked, "but even an appearance of impropriety with a subordinate is cause for immediate eyebrow raising by Ellen's family."

"That was never spelled out either," Dottie broke in. "The man may have merely wanted to help her. Angela's right. These people, with their strict codes of behavior, refused to deal with an issue head on. All this skimming over the facts leaves Ellen Olenska surrounded by a fog of disinformation and misconception. Her family doesn't want to know what had happened to Ellen, and realization of this is excruciatingly painful to her."

"Because Ellen thought that she was escaping into the loving bosom of her home town, and instead finds herself thrown to the wolves," Eliot concluded.

"Remember that illegitimacy was one of Wharton's pet themes,"

Denise pointed out. "There were no DNA tests back then. Therefore no way to prove the paternity of a child. Inheritance and heredity were major concerns. Wives had to be faithful."

"Let's get back to Newland Archer," Angela prompted, "as he is the central figure in the novel. Historians claim that *The Age of Innocence* is a portrait of a chapter in Wharton's own life—her broken engagement to Harry Stevens. The theory is that Wharton created Newland Archer as the male version of herself. She had capitulated to the stifling social forces of her implacable tribe, and separated from the man she loved."

"Yes, I agree with that analysis," I replied, "but unlike Newland Archer, Edith Wharton *did* escape, to Paris and a life of art, just as Countess Olenska does at the end of the story."

Angela grinned. "You're right, Em. I stand corrected. So, back to poor Newland, who suffers from powerful swings of emotion regarding the exotic, cultivated Ellen and her cousin, the placid, respectable May."

"He never does have sex with the Countess," Eliot scoffed. "He just thinks about it. For *years*."

"And he marries May," Denise reminded us.

Angela continued. "The upper middle class families in Wharton's New York have socialized with each other for generations, and are usually related at some level. Newland knew Ellen as a girl. He is now married to May, who is a talented horsewoman and a sure shot in archery competitions—which, according to one of the characters, is the only kind of target that she'll ever hit."

We all laughed.

"Newland is obviously bored by May and the sterile conformity of society in general. At the same time he is captivated by Ellen, who flouts convention and behaves as she pleases. She attends unfashionable parties, is seen on Fifth Avenue with questionable characters, and lives on a street which is home to professional writers. Not the thing! Perhaps Newland sees Ellen as a symbol of freedom and individuality—what he could attain if he had the courage."

"Which he doesn't," Dottie said. "He's trapped."

"What about Ellen and May's grandmother, the colossal Mrs. Mingott?" Eliot demanded. "She waffles. In the beginning she's Ellen's champion, and then suddenly she's pushing for Ellen to return to her ghastly husband, all the while practically throwing her at Newland, who's engaged to May. The old broad gave me a headache. She couldn't take a position and stick to it."

"The power of the tribe," Dottie returned, shrugging her shoulders. "Even strong willed, free thinking Granny couldn't face the force of her social circle's displeasure at Ellen's behavior. She caved."

I took advantage of a lull. "To my mind, the most astounding aspect of Wharton's novel is the fact that without uttering a word to either Ellen or Newland, the tribe silently, inexorably, conspires to divide the lovers, and pushes the unwanted Ellen out of their lives and back to Europe."

"And Newland doesn't do a blessed thing to stop them," Eliot remarked.

"He allows the forbidding hierarchy of society to make up his mind, so he doesn't have to. In the end he can't handle the tension, and he takes the easy road."

"Behind all that deadly, insincere courtesy," Dottie concluded, "the tribe has succeeded—the act of destruction is executed."

We all shivered.

"Do we agree with Old New York's verdict?" Angela asked. "Do we believe that the integrity of the social order, and its precarious balance, is more important, has more value, than an individual's desire for happiness and fulfillment? Do we hold with the concept of personal sacrifice for the public benefit? That the needs of the many outweigh the needs of the few, or the one?"

"For some stupid status war? No," Eliot replied, a little bitterly.

"Absolutely not," Denise agreed. "The public is, after all, made up of individuals. We're not talking about life and death struggles here. Separately and collectively, we all have a right to be satisfied with our lives."

"I agree," Dottie said. "A chain is only as strong as its weakest link."

"Emma?"

"As you said Ange, I think it's a precarious balance. As an observer of teenaged prep students, I can tell you that even in the twenty-first century, hidebound repression exists in the most unlikely places. And the needs of the one are utterly ignored if exposing the problem will shake that balance. The tribe must stand together, or the system collapses."

"Then you're all about sacrifice for the so-called higher good?" Eliot exclaimed in disbelief. "You're siding with the hierarchy of social order?"

"On the contrary," I said, quietly. "I'm terrified of people who do. They have no rules regarding boundaries of behavior, they're operating on pure fear, and are therefore capable of anything."

CHAPTER FOUR

Terry's Problem

Monday was a busy day for litigation lawyers. Besides short calendar, there was always the nightmare of which client did what to whom over the weekend. I had two relief from abuse petitions to defend, as well as the usual pre and post judgment motions.

Denise had called an emergency office meeting for three o'clock.

"I don't know if I'll be back in time," I said to Annie, as I shoved files in my briefcase and checked my watch. "So please take notes."

"Don't worry. I've got it covered." Annie loved office meetings. The drama generated kept her going for days.

"Is there any word on the dire issue for this afternoon?"

"None at all. Very mysterious." She licked her lips.

Connecticut General Statutes section 46b-15 provided, in part, that anyone who has been subjected to the continuous threat of present physical pain or injury, by a family member, may make application to the Superior Court for an order of relief.

Rocco Fiore was on the stand.

"I've read your affidavit, Mr. Fiore," the judge noted. "You say that your wife came after you with a baseball bat?"

"Yes, your honor."

"And that she's done this regularly in the past?"

"Yes, your honor. She sleeps with it under her bed."

"Anything to add, Ms. Carbury?"

"Mr. Fiore filed for divorce three months ago, your honor. The children of the marriage are grown and out of the house. Perhaps it would be safer for both parties if Mr. Fiore moved in with his sister for the time being."

"Is that a viable option, Mr. Fiore?"

"Yes your honor. It would be better if my wife was kept at a distance. She can be temperamental." He regarded Judge Carapresso thoughtfully. "We're Italian, you know."

I ran into Tina Rosen in the courthouse lobby.

"Do you have time for lunch?" Tina asked. "I see that we're both on the calendar for two o'clock."

We crowded in to the deli where half of the Bridgeport Bar was ordering sandwiches.

"Did you hear about what's happening to Judge Stevenson?"

I paused, tuna on a hard roll hovering in mid air. "No. What?"

"He's going in front of Judicial Review next month. It's supposed to be hush hush, so of course the entire CBA knows about it."

"Conflict of interest?"

"Nope. Sleeping with a clerk. Her husband filed the complaint."

I didn't get back to Westport until four-thirty. Annie was in my office, panting to download information.

"Judge Terrence Stevenson."

I froze.

"What about him?"

"The hearing's in a few weeks."

"I know. I just heard."

"You used to date the judge, right?" Oh Lord.

"Years ago. Why?"

"You're going to be subpoenaed to testify."

I marched into Denise's office. Luckily for her, Dottie was in the room.

"Hey partner! I can't believe I wasn't told about this in private first. I have to hear about it from my assistant, after the rest of the staff has been filled in?"

Denise was taken aback. "I just found out early this morning Em. You were still on the road, I was in court until noon, and I didn't know what your schedule was today." She paused. "When exactly were you involved with the Honorable Stevenson?"

"At least a year before I started dating Nick," I retorted, still furious. "Neither of us was married at the time."

"No, of course not," Dottie said soothingly.

"I fail to see why my personal life of nearly fifteen years ago is relevant in the present matter."

"You were his clerk, right?"

"Not when we started going out. I was an associate in the Fairfield firm by then."

"Somehow Judicial Review found out about your relationship. They're sending their investigator here on Thursday to interview you."

"Fine. I just need to know how my name got up to Hartford in connection with Terry Stevenson. Who is the clerk whose husband is complaining?"

"Arlene Pierce," Denise replied, a little sadly. "I believe you know her."

Angela met me for a drink after work.

"Who is this female?" She asked.

"Arlene was a clerk in Bridgeport. She came on board after I left to go into private practice. She has her own office in Stratford now. You remember Terry. The nicest guy on the planet. Total workaholic, which is probably why we didn't get married."

"Your sister said it was because you were too much for him. You scared him off."

"She's probably right. Terry is a gentle, kind soul. It wouldn't occur to him to hurt another human being."

"Does this Arlene have some kind of ax to grind? What's she like?"

"Strange. She went to law school later in life. Specializes in sex abuse cases. Wears black or dark purple all the time. Her hair is a big jet colored bush. Her weight goes from slim to ox and back again at regular intervals."

"What about her husband? You said that *he* filed the complaint. Was Arlene married while she was a clerk?"

"Yes. I dimly recall that he's a CPA. One of those controlling detail freaks."

"So his wife makes up an affair and he reports it to the State? Years after the fact? Does that seem normal to you?"

"What's really scary is that it all seems perfectly probable to the Judicial Review Council."

"Well, I think that you should say all of this to the investigator on Thursday. Get some ideas rolling in his mind. Arlene sounds like a psycho to me."

"Good idea. And I have to think of some discreet way to get word to Terry. If I call the courthouse, some state employed flunkie will blab, and it will be all over the internet in minutes."

"Is that wise?" Angela asked. "I thought it was your mission in life to avoid drama."

"It is. But if I can help Terry, I'm going to."

I got a call from Terry Stevenson on my cell two days later.

"Emma! Thanks for your kind note."

"Of course. I took a chance that even the courthouse staff would balk at opening a card marked 'Personal.' How are you doing?"

"I've been better, frankly. I don't understand all this. The timing couldn't be worse."

"Because you're up for reappointment?"

"Yes. I'm dealing with two committees simultaneously."

Witch hunt.

"I would imagine that she planned it that way."

"But why? Arlene was just one of the clerks. We all ate lunch together. We occasionally sat at the same table for Bar Association functions. She has been before me a few times since she went into private practice. I never felt that I had to recuse myself from her cases. I really don't know much about her."

"Was she working at the courthouse at the same time that you and I were dating?"

"Must have been. She was hired to replace you."

"Was it common knowledge that we were an item?"

"Among the judges, it was. One of them may have told Arlene." Judge Stevenson lowered his voice. "I'm sorry that you're getting dragged into this, Emma."

"I want to help, Terry. Did she ever try to hit on you?"

"Not that I'm aware of. I'll think about it, though. She wasn't even here a year."

Joanne and I were teaching Joy to canter a ten meter circle. This exercise demanded total concentration on my part. I used my inside leg against Joy's flank to maintain the bend, and the outside rein straight back, but soft, to create a wall of support. I lengthened my torso, and sat as quietly as I could, gluing my butt to my jumping saddle. Joy had to have boundaries in work, or she behaved as she pleased, usually to my detriment.

"Remember to challenge her before she challenges you!" Joanne shouted, as one of the jumper riders hurtled over an oxer and careened within a yard of us. The new trainer, Frank Shaw, disparaging to everyone in the ring—even his clients, gave me a disgusted look, and waved his student over for a consult.

Joy expressed her displeasure by standing up on her back legs, pinning her ears to her head, and sneering at her equine counterpart.

"Not your fault, Emma," Joanne said, quietly. "There's no reason for Frank to use every jump in this ring for one student. There's plenty of space."

"He's a bully," I growled, in reply. "He gets off on ramming his out of control horses into everyone else. It's an intimidation tactic. He's lucky someone hasn't gotten hurt."

"Frank says dressage is for pansies who are afraid to jump," Joanne remarked, "which is ridiculous. It takes an unbelievable amount of focus to keep a horse in a package like you're doing."

"I've done jumper courses, remember," I said, hopping off. "And I can tell you that I've never been able to ride this well before. Dressage is exhausting! I can barely last through half of my lesson. Being precise and making it look beautiful requires a lot of energy."

I led Joy to the mounting block so Joanne could finish the hour.

Joanne showed her horses at the fourth level, and being new to this discipline, I was still in awe of her incredible talent. I watched Joanne and Joy execute perfect half passes at the canter in both directions, and then move on to tempe changes—flying lead changes that swapped back and forth—like skipping. With only a few months of dressage work, Joy was doing one tempes with ease.

"Joy is a phenomenal athlete, as you know Emma," Joanne

remarked, dismounting after half an hour. "Her power and balance are amazing. Unfortunately, she's also super smart. Riding her is definitely an adventure."

I happened to glance over at Frank as Joanne was speaking. He had clearly been watching Joy's performance, which for some reason, made me extremely uneasy.

That night I dreamed that I am cantering on Merriment through the pastureland on the far side of the Hunterbury River. I am wearing my deep blue riding habit with the full skirt, which I know is very flattering to my figure. It also brightens the blue of my eyes. Zachary has said so, and I am wearing it especially for him. Merry jumps the fence neatly, and we trot to the small grove of trees near Sinclair's farm.

Zachary is waiting at the usual place, under the big beech tree, astride his gray stallion. "Hannah!" He cries, leaping down. "I was beginning to fear that you would not come today."

"Joshua is asking questions again, and I am worried that he is watching me." I dismount, and leave Merry to graze. "But I found that I could not miss this chance to see you."

"I am very glad," he says, taking my hand. "Have you thought anymore about my proposal?"

In my mind I am able to see us escaping to Boston together, but I shake my head.

"But why not?" Zachary exclaims. "My brother will help us—he has work for me. We would be free, Hannah!"

"Not one of us is free until this war is finished. You know that. I am afraid to go, Zack. I am afraid of a life as a married woman, living with a man who is not my husband. Boston is not so very far. It would never be right; I would always be ashamed, and you and I should be miserable. You would grow to regret your choice."

He drops my hand. A black cloud moves over his face.

"While your husband lives. As you say, we are at war. Death is common place."

I am aware that he is angry. But Zachary is a good man. "You know that I am right. My decision is not for lack of true feeling! Tis heaven to be with you! But I can not go against my marriage vow."

Zachary moves quickly back to his stallion and leaps into the saddle. "I question a vow that forces you to stay with a man who is not kind to you," he says bitterly, turning his horse toward town. "With me it is the opposite. Happiness is not a privilege. It is a right. Why else should we defend ourselves against an oppressive ruler as we do? General Washington has ordered the Connecticut militia to march. The word is that Washington expects the arrival of the French fleet under Admiral d'Estaing. The General wants to take back New York. I am going Hannah."

Fear chokes my throat. "Then I may lose you," I say, my hand on his arm.

There is disdain in his face now. "Win or lose, we have to fight. I will never give up."

I watch him gallop away, knowing that he will head north, away from his law practice—to his farm at the foot of the hills.

CHAPTER FIVE

Love List

Carlie and I collected our art equipment and proceeded down to the edge of the dock. As my property was situated on a peninsula, we had water views on three sides of us. To our right was the Hunterbury River, with the Woodruff Bridge out of sight to the north. In front of us, the large expanse of Lake Washington, with the point of its largest island on our left. We set up our easels and folding chairs, and adjusted our umbrellas to block the glare of the sun.

The fall foliage had begun to present itself. My first autumn in Litchfield County was going to be glorious.

"Look at that heron!" Carlie pointed. "It's huge! I hope he'll stand still long enough for me to paint him."

"Are you getting excited about school?" I asked. "This is a big change from a hometown high school in rural Vermont."

"I'm totally excited!" Carlie replied. "I love my classes, and rowing, and the teachers are amazing! I'm even making some friends. But I'm a little worried about my family. My big sister has started at UVM, so it's just my parents home alone on the farm now. It will be tough on Mom. Everything's changing."

"There are so many reasons that I chose not to have kids, but having to let go of one's brood eventually has got to be one of them. Animals, after all, stay with you."

"Yeah," Carlie agreed. "They just don't live as long."

One of the challenges of painting outdoors was that light and shadow were constantly shifting. Working in a studio with a specific photographic reference was much easier, but somehow less satisfying.

"Notice how the clouds coming in have affected the colors in the water. See the reds and oranges and yellows? I'll show you some techniques for painting reflections. Look at the darker values at the edge of the bank all around the lake, especially on this side of the island," I instructed. "Your heron hasn't found anything tasty. He's hardly moved."

"Emma," Carlie began. "What's the deal with your family? You never talk about them. Well," she grinned, "I've heard you say some pretty funny things about your mother. Is it true that you never had kids because she was so miserable to you?"

"I don't know," I replied. "I have a whole list of excuses, really. Mostly I just didn't want any more responsibility, or sacrifice. I'm determined to spend the bulk of my adult life having a great childhood. Freedom is a wonderful thing."

"But don't you get lonely? You've had two husbands, right? Don't you miss having someone else around? Isn't living alone a little scary?"

"But I'm never alone!" I indicated Abby, sprawled on a steamer chair, asleep. "My animals are terrific company. They're amusing, smart, sensitive, and one hundred percent loyal. What could be better than that?"

Carlie shifted gears. "OK. So what happened with your first marriage?"

"It was a long time ago. I had a terrible job with the state that paid almost nothing, and no benefits. The economy was in bad shape. Young lawyers were taking secretarial and paralegal positions just to pay the rent. Shawn was a junior partner at a firm in Westport, doing real estate and some litigation. We were only married for a couple of years, and spent at least half of that time apart."

"Did he cheat?"

"Big time. With women, and with money. Everyone, including my sister, kept telling me that Shawn was unfaithful, but I refused to believe it. In the end, he left me with an apartment in Trumbull that he knew I couldn't afford on my own, and went back to Westport to sponge off his wealthy grandmother. I eventually got evicted. I had to put most of my belongings in storage and live in house sharing situations with total strangers, while working two jobs. This went on for about three years, until I got the job with the Fairfield firm, and eventually moved in with Nick. Then the economy picked up, and I made partner."

"Your parents wouldn't help?"

"Dad wanted to. But he was semi retired and Audrey controlled the money." I paused, laughing. "Interesting, the things you remember. My tires were bald, it was winter, and Dad had to sneak me cash from a machine so Audrey wouldn't find out that he had bought me new ones."

"Why was your mom so mean? Mothers are supposed to be generous and loving."

"Hah! Two words in the English language that I would *never* use to describe Audrey. It's like the title of a country song. 'I used to think she's evil, but now I know she's just a fool.' The woman is so impossibly self centered that it would never occur to her to extend herself for another human being. On the contrary. Other people are here to do for her." I was thoughtful for a moment. "I think there was an element of jealousy as well. Audrey may have been enjoying the power imbalance—me on the bottom, for a change."

"So, is that why you didn't have children?"

"Because I was afraid that I'd be as ghastly at motherhood as Audrey was? Possible. I really like my independence, and I have a very comfortable lifestyle now. There's Joy, and Abby, all my friends and clients. This house. Teaching. Hobbies. They keep me busy." I paused. "I'd really love to do less driving back and forth to the coast, but that will come."

"But wouldn't you like a man now? Not a husband, maybe. But kind of a BFF with benefits?" Carlie looked at me slyly. "You know. Sex?"

"What do you know about sex?" I demanded. Should someone be screening her Facebook account?

"Just what I read, and see in movies and TV," she replied carefully. "I'm guessing that if it wasn't so great, people wouldn't be trying so hard to do it all the time."

"Hmm. Nice save," I said. "Very smooth. Sure. I'd love to meet the guy of my dreams. But he'd have to be some incredible kind of man. Really smart, kind, funny, adventurous. Good judgment. Outdoor sports. A whole lot of character would be nice. I have so had it with phony charm." I mused a bit. "Complete absence of family drama would be a bonus. Cooking skills."

"So why don't you make a list?" Carlie asked, practically. "Aren't you always telling me that if I want something, write it down, and send it out there somehow? What are you afraid of? Another Nick?"

I put down my brush. "How did you get so smart? Were you always like this?"

Carlie rolled her eyes at me. "Uh, yeah. I told you. I read. I've been looking through your witchcraft books. Why don't you just cast a spell?"

An hour later we were back in the house, discussing dinner options.

"How about we get going on bringing in my Soul Mate?"

"Now?" Carlie bellowed. "But I'm starving!"

"Hey, you wanted me to do this! Start looking at all the love energy stuff, and I'll order a pizza."

Carlie piled the books on the library table and started going through indexes, taking notes.

"So far I've got candles, apples, roses...."

"Pink, or red?"

"Um, red is physical passion, pink is for romantic love."

"Better get both. Next?"

"Garnets, rose quartz, emeralds and carnelian, whatever that is. Jade."

"I've got a garnet bracelet, and rose quartz earrings. Some jade charms."

"Love herbs and spices are lavender, rosemary, chamomile and cinnamon, cloves, nutmeg."

"I'm either growing them, or they're on a shelf in the kitchen."

"Timing is important," Carlie continued. "Time of day, days of the week, phases of the moon. Friday is Venus day, so best for love spells. Sunrise to mid day to start new relationships, and a waxing or full moon." Carlie looked up. "You know what Emma? You really should get a Book of Shadows, so it'll be easy to find this info when you want it. All of these resources say to do things a little differently. You need to discover what works for you, and record it."

"OK. You can start your own too. Keep reading."

"There's a lot here about poppets," she said, holding up an illustration. "They look kind of like voodoo dolls."

"Put a tab on those pages. I'll read them later."

"Make a list of the qualities you want in your new man, using positive terms only. Tell the Universe what you want, not what you don't want."

"So, I should ask for tall, rather than not short?"

"Exactly."

"Here's what I've got so far," I said.

Male
Caucasian
Forty to Fifty-five
Five eleven or taller
Intelligent and intellectual
Capable of interesting conversation
Honest, dependable, reliable
Emotionally available for a long term relationship
Capable of emotional separation from family
        of origin
Free from organized religion
Funny and fun
Physically attractive to me
Excellent lover
Attractive voice
Romantic
Articulate
Affectionate
Generous with money and time
Emotionally stable
Grounded and sensible
Emotionally secure
Healthy, physically strong, and athletic
Gentle
Financially independent
Tidy, neat in dress and living habits
Respectful and respect worthy
Loves outdoors, outdoor sports, and animals
Enjoys foreign travel and adventure

Lives in or within an hour's drive from
Western Connecticut
Free from parenting responsibilities
Capable of and enjoys cooking meals

"This is pretty intense, Emma. Do you think there's a guy that great around here?"

I shrugged. "There has to be, or close enough, anyway. It's what I want, and Sophie swears that magick works."

"Then I think we should do this right. I vote we go over there tomorrow, and buy the proper ingredients. All the stones and herbs and stuff. The books say that magick is all about energy, so let's make it special."

"OK. I've always wanted my own cauldron. Seems appropriate, somehow."

"While we're at it," Carlie made a face. "Let's ask about poppets."

Saturday morning, after a big breakfast at Nancy's Diner, Carlie and I proceeded to *Root and Branch*, Sophie Sullivan's garden store. Her daughter informed us that Sophie was in the greenhouse, tending her potted herbs.

I was hesitant about broaching the subject of witchcraft, but Carlie jumped right in.

"We need an athame, a censor and some other things," she announced, referring to her list. "Stones, a pentacle, candles, various herbs. A Book of Shadows for each of us. Oh, and a cauldron for Emma."

Sophie washed her hands in the sink by the potting bench, called to Julie to mind the shop, and beckoned us to a large white shed at the back of the property.

"People have to inquire to be brought here," she explained. "I've had some trouble with the locals, and I don't want Julie exposed to that kind of venomous energy." She opened the door and stepped back. "Feel free to look around," she invited.

"Wow!" Carlie exclaimed.

I had imagined a gloomy chamber, like the Halliwell sisters' attic in *Charmed*, but instead, was introduced to several small rooms, light and cheerful in feeling. The sun streamed in from three skylights, and from French doors at either end of the shed.

"Wiccans revere nature," Sophie said. "The seasons, animals, trees and plants. We celebrate a joyful life. I call this room my magickal pantry. You should find every herb you need here." There were three walls entirely shelved with rows and rows of labeled jars. "This area," Sophie continued "will address your altar needs. I would advise you to just get a few of the basics. Witches love to buy magickal toys, but they rarely use most of them. By the way, never lend your tools, and never borrow them from someone else. Most importantly, know that the power doesn't come from tools like magick wands. It comes from inside of each of us."

Carlie picked out a simple ritual athame—a double edged dull blade with a triquetra trinity knot on its black handle. I found a small cast iron lidded cauldron with a pentacle raised on the front, and an incense burner, or censor, with a chain. We each selected large black leather bound books, with plain covers, and three ribbon markers sewn in.

"The masculine and the feminine are now represented on your altar," Sophie beamed.

"I already have these items, from my shamanic days," I said, looking at the small selection of drums, rattles, and feather fans.

"It's all the same, really," Sophie said. "Raising, and moving energy in an altered state of consciousness. All religions came from

Shamanism. I find the Wiccan way of life to be softer, more feminine. It works for me. We all have to find what fits."

Carlie was eyeing the jewelry section. I steered her toward a corner where shelves of glass bowls were filled with small polished stones.

"Amethyst, citron, garnet, topaz, turquoise," Carlie read from the labels.

"I'll get the pink candles. Oh wow, rose incense!"

"Emma needs to find a man," Carlie explained to Sophie. "So we're going to summon her one. She's only dated one guy since she left her husband. A judge. And that didn't last very long."

"Golf and tennis," I said, by way of explanation.

Sophie laughed. "Ah yes. Men do enjoy their competitive games. Well, my advice is Keep it Simple. I find that the less complicated the spell is, the better it works." She handed us each a folded flyer. "My witchcraft classes start in a few weeks. Just in case you're interested."

CHAPTER SIX

Bullying

The Connecticut Alliance of Professional Women was sponsoring a series of talks at the Ludlow Public Library. Open to the public and free of charge, our mission was encouraging people, especially women and teens, to raise their level of awareness regarding emotionally charged issues. We covered topics such as financial power and devaluing in relationships, incest, and bullying.

As Co-Chairs, Denise and I took turns setting up and running these events. Our speakers were members of the group who were interested in sharing their expertise.

On Thursday evening, Miranda Pollack, Ph.D. was addressing the audience on the subject of bullying in schools.

"Bullying is learned behavior," Randy began. "It involves deliberate, willful actions, calculated to harm, and to induce terror of retaliation if the target tells. In turn, the bully takes pleasure in the pain that he or she is inflicting. These people have no fear of punishment, and they are assured that bystanders will do nothing to intervene.

"My focus will be what is going on right now in the schools, but I want to make it clear that this research applies equally to adults—in relationships, friendships, and even in the workplace. Bullying does not end with adolescence. On the contrary, unchecked behavior continues, and often children who were bullied evolve into adults who bully others, even their own kids.

"The key ingredient is an imbalance of power. The discrepancies between the aggressor and the victim may be obvious, such as size and athletic ability, or they may be something much more subtle. If you came here tonight believing that bullying always includes physical violence, I guarantee that you will leave with new information in your tool box.

"We hear about physical bullying in the media all of the time. Horrific tragedies like Columbine High School and Virginia Tech, and stories of victim suicides, now called bullycides, always catch the public eye.

"But physical acts are only one form of bullying, and although it is more common among males to inflict bodily harm on victims, this is no longer exclusively male behavior.

"Verbal bullying is practiced by both genders, and can be equally toxic, even without physical injury. Evidence can be overheard, or read.

"Relationship bullying is practiced mostly by females, and it is almost impossible to detect by an outsider.

"The reason for this is that boys tend to congregate in large, loose groups, usually athletic in nature. They value physical skill and strength over intellectual ability, and are constantly vying for the alpha position. This is why negative epithets such as fag, wimp, nerd, or sissy are so damaging to a boy's self esteem. It is very important to note that a hierarchy such as this places girls on the lowest level of the totem pole in terms of power and respect.

"Which in turn explains a great deal about adult behavior such as spousal abuse, and child sexual abuse."

There was an audible ripple of enlightenment in the audience.

"Girls, in contrast, prefer small intimate groups with hierarchies and boundaries firmly in place. Females develop their sense of self, and self worth through their relationships with others, especially peers. They are much more inclined to deeper emotional connections, and socializing.

"Modern girls are bombarded with information. The Web, magazines, television, movies—even music. Our culture is telling them that they must be thin, dress provocatively, have boyfriends, get good grades, and excel at athletic competitions. Compounding this problem is the fact that girls are physically maturing much earlier than previous generations. They are mini Venus archetypes, without the emotional wherewithal to handle the consequences. Their role models are anorexic rock stars whose personal dysfunctions are splayed across the Internet every day.

"As a result, girls today are part of a culture that promotes competitiveness, sameness, and a pecking order in social relationships, known as cliques. Competitiveness generates adversaries, and trust is impossible.

"At the same time, girls are seeking independence from their parents, and establishing themselves among their peers as young adults.

"Therefore, shunning a girl from a particular group can be traumatizing in the extreme.

"How is this accomplished?

"In school, on the bus, or at school related events, the behavior can be eye rolling, name calling, whispering, ridiculing, taunting, ostracizing. Cruel comments regarding the victim's appearance and body. Notes passed, or left in the locker of the target. Threats of physical injury, or death.

"Attacks regarding the target's sexuality are particularly virulent.

"Outside school the harassment can take the form of stalking, crank calls, and spreading disinformation or rumors, via the Internet, or texting. The latter is known as cyberbullying. The abuse may be comments on a Facebook page, surveys on web sites, videos on YouTube, pornographic photos on cell phones, stealing a victim's screen name to stir up chaos, tricking the target into revealing secrets—and then posting them on the Web, or a dozen other variations.

"The big problems with cyberbullying are first, that the damage is usually anonymous, so the bully doesn't see or hear the immediate effects. This lessens any feelings of remorse or guilt. Also, there are many more witnesses who are seeing the results. The victim feels as though there is no escape. Moreover, it is very difficult to hold the school accountable, as the action does not take place on school property.

"The traditional concept that bullying only occurs when boys in leather jackets gang up on the skinniest kid in the class is outdated, and frankly ignorant. Emotional violence is subtle, insidious, and much more difficult to track to the source. Mean girls know how to attack the self esteem of their prey, striking the victim's identity at its deepest level. The object is to generate as much drama as they can, without getting caught.

"Children who have been victims of the 'girl poisoning' culture, or any form of protracted bullying, usually suffer from chronic trauma, known as Post Traumatic Stress Disorder. PTSD manifests as depression, anxiety, addictions, compulsive behavior, and eating disorders. Sometimes the rage builds up until the target explodes, and she acts out of character. I've seen model students suddenly cutting classes, cheating on tests, damaging school property, and even physically attacking the bully. And yes, I have dealt with cases of bullycide as a result of relationship aggression in my practice. All of these reactions are screams for help. These kids believe that nothing can be done to stop their tormentors.

"Unfortunately, many adults still aren't listening, and many of the schools just don't get it. 'Boys will be boys,' they claim. And 'girls will be girls.'

"Any questions so far?"

A sea of hands appeared. A young woman in the second row stood up.

"How does a bully choose his or her target?"

"That's a very important question, thank you. I should have covered that. Victims of bullying are usually kids who don't fit in. Sometimes they are what we call 'provocative,' meaning that there are obvious differences that include race, religion, physical or learning challenges. Sexuality issues. Sometimes the child is generating jealousy—she might be new to the school, or an excellent student, or she is dating a popular boy and the other girls are envious.

"Bullies are careful—remember, they don't want to get caught. They test the waters with a target, first to ascertain whether or not the victim will fight back or tell, and second to see if any bystanders will protect this person. The behavior might begin with a casual taunt thrown out, or a surreptitious shove in the hall. If there is no reaction, the harassment will escalate. Bullies have an innate genius for picking on people who have low self esteem, and aren't likely to defend themselves.

"Which brings me to the next point. How do you know when a child is being bullied, if there are no cuts or bruises visible on the outside? The most common indicators are sudden loss of interest in school, unprecedented drop in grades, quitting favorite activities, faked illnesses, and expressing the wish to either drop out or be home schooled."

Another question. "What's the deal with bystanders? Why do so few students step up to the plate?"

Randy laughed. "That query could apply to most of humanity, don't you think? The answer is simple. Fear. Fear of retaliation, or fear of loss of status with the bully. It takes tremendous courage to stand up to power."

A man in the back raised his hand. "What about the schools? Why is it so difficult for worried parents to get help?"

"School administrators, especially those in private schools, are famous for insulating themselves from the rest of the world. If a complaint is made, the people at the top invariably minimize the problem and resort to defensive mode, shunning the victimized child and her parents in the process. They'll do anything to keep the story quiet.

"When one is dealing with a private school, this reaction is magnified. Contrary to popular belief, big tuition bills do not guarantee control of your child's environment. Often the opposite is the case. Private schools are not receiving public funding, and are very likely to show you the door if there is a problem. Their boards have no statutory obligation to educate a child."

"But they *are* under contract, right?" The man exclaimed. "When they take our money, they have a legal duty, express or implied, to educate our kids, and to keep them safe."

"Absolutely. If the administration and the school board refuse to help, I'm afraid the only recourse is to hire a lawyer. I've testified in court cases where financial awards were made for physical and emotional injury as a result of bullying in private schools, as well as tuition reimbursement. New law is slow, but it will happen. Bravery—and a commitment to making things right—are always the first steps toward positive change.

"A final word about bullying," Randy continued. "On a small scale it does enough damage. On a community, or even national scale, the results are horrific. Consider what history has taught us—Christians thrown to the lions by the Romans, Catholics hunted down by Protestants. Wise women tortured, hanged and burned by governments who claimed they were witches in league

with the devil. Mass beheadings of aristocrats by French peas-
ants. And more recently, Hitler's near annihilation of the Jews in
Europe.

"Atrocities such as these occur only when there is a power imbalance, and bystanders don't have the courage to take action. Think
about it."

I dragged myself out of bed at five thirty on Saturday morning
for Masters Rowing practice. It was unusually chilly for September,
and as I pulled on my black Lycra pants, I considered the retribu-
tion I might exact upon Carlie for forcing me into this misery.

At just before six the BHS boathouse was swarming with adults
wearing high visibility jackets, hauling fours and eights down to
the dock. The captain, Art Blakesley, a civil engineer, waved me
over.

"The women are all set in their boats Emma," he announced.
"So if you don't mind, I'm going to put you in the eight with the
men. We're down a few members today, and no coxswain. Business
trips—so you'd really be helping us out."

He indicated a group of gentlemen near the oar rack. Not one
of them stood less than six foot two. And they were all gods.

I was placed just ahead of the bow position in the boat.

Suddenly, there was Carlie on the dock, waving her camera, and
giving me a big grinning thumbs up. I visualized her having dinner alone with my mother and sister, as we pushed off and moved
down river toward the lake.

"Emma's a trial lawyer," Art announced to the crew, as we set
an initially leisurely pace. Not comfortable with sweep—using one
oar, I had to stay focused. "She's new to the area, and teaching a
class on Evidence at BHS."

"Henry Judson," yelled the man in the bow, behind me.
"Portfolio manager. My daughter's a freshman at TA."

"Luke MacLaren," the Adonis in front of me hollered. "I'm a landscape architect, and a BHS alum."

A chorus of names came back toward me in the breeze, like a Gregorian chant. Will Kirby, restaurant owner, son and daughter both rowing. Phil Deming—in stroke position, construction company owner, another alum. Karl Skinner, child psychiatrist in town, on the TA board. Max Feeney, physical therapy group partner.

It was a hard row. Art began to set drills as soon as we cleared the beach area, and the strokes per minute rose, faster and faster. Hampered by shorter arms and legs and less weight, I did my best to keep up with the rhythm. I was frankly exhausted an hour later, when we finally came full circle, and Henry steered us into the dock.

We stepped out of the eight, and released our oars from the riggers.

"Toes over the edge!" Art called. We positioned ourselves to lift the heavy boat out of the water and flip it. Used to doubles and singles at the Westport club, the weight was almost too much for me.

"Take this, Emma," Will said, handing me a folded towel. "It will ease the strain going up the ramp."

I shoved the yellow towel under the gunwale that was crushing my right shoulder—the relief was enormous.

On the patio the women had set up coffee cake and mimosas.

I tried to keep track of names, but gave up almost immediately. I accepted a glass gratefully from one of the ladies. No sign of Carlie. She must have gone back to bed.

"Excellent job Emma!" Max said. "Pretty tough being thrown in with us your first time out."

"You've got terrific balance," Henry added. "It really helped me with the steering. A refreshing change."

"You had Fred's position—he's in Montreal this weekend," Art explained, in a low voice. "Fred's new to rowing, and not the fittest member of the team."

"I keep my mare just outside of town," I said. "Riding is all about balance, and rowing shells, unlike horses, are never capricious. A lot less stress."

"That explains it," Luke put in, filling my empty glass.

"What?"

"Your form. You're very controlled and graceful. The mark of a true athlete."

I stared at him. He smiled gently, and moved away to speak to Dan and Karl.

CHAPTER SEVEN

Protectors and
Enforcers of Tradition

"Today we're going to talk about the plot of Jane Austen's *Pride and Prejudice*," I reminded my Evidence class. "Not, however, from the literary perspective. You've all watched some version of the movie for homework, right? Remember that the legal definition of hearsay is 'an out of court statement repeated in court for the purpose of proving that what the declarant said is true.' For our purposes we will not be operating in a courtroom, but in Hertfordshire, England, in the late eighteenth century.

"The title of Austen's most famous novel is a clue. To which of her characters does the word 'prejudice' refer?"

Lexie raised her hand. "Elizabeth Bennet."

"Good. Why?"

Lexie again. "Because she believes George Wickham's story about Mr. Darcy without conducting a background check."

"Excellent Alexandra. Let's dig deeper. Who wants to give us a brief synopsis of Mr. Wickham's sad narrative?"

"He claims to have been cheated out of a career in the church by Fitzwilliam Darcy," Ted replied. "He also tells Lizzy that Darcy's sister Georgiana is a spoiled waste of space."

Laughter.

"A little caustic, but concise. Why is Elizabeth so quick to take Wickham's tale to heart?"

Paul waved his right arm. "Because Darcy refused to dance with her at the beginning of the book."

"You would say that!" Lexie exclaimed, outraged.

"Ms. Doyle, you have a comment?" I asked, sweetly.

"Darcy is abysmally rude to Elizabeth at the first ball," Lexie announced, her face flushed. "Even by today's standards." An undercurrent of whispering and bursts of laughter began to erupt from the back of the room. "He's the 'pride' part of the title, after all. It's only natural that Elizabeth would assume the worst of him!"

"Arguing from experience, Doyle?" Therese bellowed from the last row.

"Ms. Ellis, I've spoken to you about disrupting class before," I replied, even louder. There was silence in the room.

"Tell me about Caroline Bingley. What's her agenda? Why is she so condescending to Lizzy?"

"She wants to marry Darcy," Cassie answered. "And by the time of her brother's ball, she is aware of Darcy's preference for Elizabeth."

"But she also knows that Elizabeth is attracted to Wickham," Maddie added.

"So what does she do?" I prompted them.

"Miss Bingley tells Lizzy that Wickham is a lowly born scoundrel," Cassie said, "and that she should set her sights elsewhere."

"But when Lizzy presses her for specific details," Amy continued, "Miss Bingley has none."

"She has heard the entire story from her brother," Jeanne said.

"Hearsay!" Cassie concluded, triumphant.

"But Caroline Bingley is right, isn't she?" Piper demanded.

"Yeah," Paul replied. "But Elizabeth is so jaded about Darcy, and the Bingleys, that she won't listen."

"Wonderful people! You're getting this very quickly," I remarked, proud of them. "OK. So what's Wickham's agenda?"

Rob waved his pen. "The solution to Wickham's behavior has two parts. First, he wasn't banned from the church—he requested financial compensation for the living on Darcy's estate, and was granted it. Second, he then attempted to run off with Darcy's fifteen year old sister Georgiana—she had a fortune of her own—but was discovered by Darcy at the eleventh hour."

"So Wickham was trying to smear Darcy's name to get back at him!" Maddie said.

"And Elizabeth, in her anger, and ignorance, willingly spreads the story," I added. "You have now learned something about the credibility of witnesses as well. Remember that the term impeachment refers to the introduction of evidence aimed at discrediting the accuracy or truthfulness of testimony."

There was a moment while everyone processed this information. I glanced over at Lexie. Her head was bent down to her open notebook, her big glasses had slid practically off her nose, and her cheeks were bright red. She was quietly crying.

"What are some other examples of he said/she said in *Pride and Prejudice*?" I asked, quickly. "Who will tell us about Bingley's sisters and their treatment of Elizabeth's older sister, Jane?"

"Both sisters—Caroline and Mrs. Hurst—want their brother Charles to marry Darcy's sister, Georgiana," Cassie explained. "To keep it all in the family, I guess. It would give Caroline a better shot at Darcy. But it's obvious from the beginning that Charles is really into Jane."

"Jane is the quiet type," Matt continued, "she doesn't show her feelings much—and Charles is kind of a weenie. His sisters, and

Darcy, work on him. They have him convinced that Jane doesn't really like him, so he gives up trying."

"And Jane spends most of the novel hurting from his rejection," Heather explained, "until Darcy straightens him out in the end."

"Darcy finally realizes that he's been a jerk!" Cassie added.

"What a mess!" Amy concluded, shaking her head in disbelief.

"And it ain't over yet!" I replied, laughing. "Let's move on to Lady Catherine and her daughter, Anne. What's their agenda?"

"The same thing!" Ted chuckled. "Lady C wants her nephew Darcy to marry his cousin Anne—who's sickly and dull. Darcy sure is one marked man. All these women flocking around, pecking at him!"

"Except for Lizzy," Maddie retorted, "the one he wants. Only she can't stand him."

"Until after he proposes to her," Amy reminded us, "and she blows him off. Then he writes her that long letter—explaining Wickham, Georgiana, Jane and Bingley—everything."

"More hearsay," Cassie pointed out. "Darcy wants to clear his name with Elizabeth."

"Then Lizzy hears the truth about Darcy from his housekeeper, who would know," Paul said, wisely. "She says that he's basically kind, good tempered and generous. She explains that he's not proud—just quiet."

Heather snickered.

"So Queen Bee Lady Catherine marches over to Elizabeth's house," Jeanne continued, "is rude to her mother, and flatly announces to Lizzy that Darcy is engaged to her daughter Anne, thank you very much, so back off!"

"The big question," I said, when the laughter had died down, "is this: How much of Austen's plot would be left if we took out all of the hearsay?"

"Not a whole heck of a lot!" Piper said.

"And there you have the basis for most fiction!" I concluded. "Literary or not. A tangle of dramatic he said/she said, with very little attention to the facts. Good work today. Next time we will continue discussing the credibility of witnesses. Please look over your syllabus and be prepared with the materials."

They moved out of the room in groups. I sat quietly in my seat until only Lexie remained. She got up and was gathering her belongings. She did not look at me.

I moved over to the chair next to her.

"Therese Ellis was pretty tough on you, Lexie," I began, and she looked up in dismay.

"Is this going to affect my grade?" She asked, starting to cry again. She grabbed blindly at a pen that had rolled on to the floor.

"Of course not!" I told her, retrieving it. "You're one of the brightest students in this class. But I need to know if something is going on with you. Therese has a following of big athletes in the back of the room—they seem to travel in a pack. Are they bothering you?"

"I'm fine," she mumbled, heading for the door. "I just have a lot of work to do, besides track practice, and Student Government. I get really tired sometimes. Thanks."

And she was gone.

I invited Carlie and Julie to my house for afternoon tea. We sat by the water, while I poured out iced orange pekoe with mint and lemon, and passed a three tiered assortment of European pastries from Isabella's in town.

Abby strolled down to the dock and stretched out, nose on her front paws—her eyes on a family of ducks that was passing by.

The girls were chatting about school, dorm life, and their extra curricular activities, while I sat and listened. Eventually there was a pause, and Carlie looked over at me.

"Sorry, Emma. We're hogging the conversation."

"This is nice," Julie said, leaning back in her chair. "It's really quiet here. There's always so much noise and busy stuff on campus. You never get a break."

"Yeah, thanks," Carlie agreed. "Anything new with you?"

"No dates yet, if that's what you're asking."

Carlie grinned. "Just curious. That's an awfully nice group of guys for you to choose from, though. All about the right age, too." She took a bite of éclair. "I've done some checking with the Coach."

I sat up. "What kind of checking?"

"Oh, you know. Who's married. Who's single. That kind of thing."

I struggled with this information. "So?"

"I thought you'd be interested," Carlie said, pulling a sheet of paper from her backpack. "Here's the scoop. The captain—Art. He's divorced. Wife and two kids in Farmington. Henry and Will have wives, and kids who are students at TA, and/or BHS. So they're out. Dan's divorced too, but he's living with someone in Kent. Karl, the school shrink? Everyone's pretty sure that he's gay, but he keeps it quiet. But Max and Phil are available."

"What about Luke?" I asked, probably too quickly.

"Hmm. The Coach wasn't sure. Says he lives on an old family farm in Bridge Hollow, but travels a lot, because of his work. He's never seen Luke with a date—says he's quiet about his personal life. The still waters run deep kind of guy." She looked up. "I can keep digging, if you like," she offered, handing me her man research.

"That's OK," I replied, "I appreciate this, honey. Thanks."

Carlie was watching my face. "Luke huh? He's the one?"

"Something about him got to me, that's all." I looked over at Julie, who seemed to be dozing. "I need to make sure that it's a good something."

"And not just another Dump and Suck? Understood."

We sat quietly for a bit.

"Carlie," I proceeded with caution. "Please tell me about the girls' rowing captain."

Julie opened her eyes.

"Therese?" For the first time since I'd known her, I sensed hesitation, and perhaps even a little fear, in Carlie's tone.

It was Julie who took the initiative. "Tell her about the PETs, Carlie," she directed. "You've been saying that you wanted to."

Abby suddenly jumped up, growling. Her tail was moving so fast, it was a blur. A turtle had popped its head out of the water. Startled by the noise, it disappeared. Abby remained poised at the very edge of the dock, her tawny rump vibrating with indignation.

"Tell her Carlie."

"They're the Protectors and Enforcers of Tradition, Emma," she began. "Known as the PETs. Julie and I, and all the other transfers, were herded with the freshmen into a meeting in the auditorium. About a week after school started."

"It was really creepy," Julie said. "No teachers, none of the school heads. Just students. They made a big deal about closing the doors behind us, and keeping the lights low. It was all very hush hush."

"The PETs are all seniors," Carlie explained. "New recruits are tapped at the end of their junior year by the outgoing members."

"They lined up on the stage, facing us," Julie continued. "About twelve of them. They were all big girls—jocks mostly. Dressed in black, with heavy black eye makeup, and big clunky heels. Some of them even wore chains instead of belts."

I couldn't contain myself. "You're making this up!"

"Nope. I got a picture on my cell. Look." Carlie held up her phone.

It wasn't a great shot, because of the light, but the image was clear enough. A dozen dominatrix types, forming a wall of intimidation. A few rows of terrified little girls sat below them, in front of Carlie, faces registering dismay as they turned to each other in fright. In the middle, largest of all—Therese Ellis. Hands on her hips, thick legs slightly apart, as though she was going to indulge in a set of deep knee bends while she addressed the group.

"And the message?" I asked, keeping my voice cool. "What was the object of this meeting?"

"In a word—silence," Carlie replied, grimly. "We're to keep our mouths shut about everything, and anything, that goes on at Tallmadge Academy for Girls."

"And if we don't," Julie added, her eyes wide with fear, "They will make sure that we leave school."

"In pieces," Carlie said.

CHAPTER EIGHT

Lexie's Story

I drove the girls back to the dorm, promising Julie that I would let her mom know what was going on. In return, I asked them to keep quiet about this information until I'd had a chance to think. "But let me know if you see or hear anything important," I said to Carlie. "Be careful about emails. We'll keep a log, at my house. If I end up going to the administration, I want to have a record to show them. Please watch your back. And send that photo to me."

Not altogether thrilled with the idea of Carlie playing spy with that band of harpies, I drove back home, and took a glass of chardonnay to a steamer chair near the water. Abby stretched out across my knees.

The sun was setting earlier these days—a nice breeze ruffled Abby's fur, and created a symmetric ripple in the water. I dozed off.

Christopher walks slowly into my herb room, his small frame shaking with anger. His face is covered in a layer of dirt mixed with blood. I rise from my table without a word to him, and pour water into the big white basin. With a rag I begin to clean his face and hands.

"The boys again?" I ask, and he nods, wincing with the pain.

"They claim that my brother is a traitor." He spits out the words. "They swear they will kill me for it."

"I have worried about William myself, Christopher. He left his studies at this school to write for a Loyalist newspaper. He is in New York with the British."

"Will hates the King!"

His voice is thick, and difficult to understand. I soon discover that he has lost teeth. I mix a small quantity of salt with some water, and have him rinse his mouth several times. I treat his open wounds and his pain and soreness of muscles.

Once Christopher has left me, I sit at my writing table and open my book. I dip the quill in ink and make the proper notations.

20th September 1779 ~ to Christopher Marsh

Wounds ~ hot compress of two teaspoons of Balm leaves boiled in water ten minutes. Strained leaves. Applied with a clean cloth.
Sore Muscles and Ache ~ tincture of Meadowsweet ~ advised him to return if Nausea occurs.

I close my book, and hide it in its usual place; behind the wall of the cupboard. Joshua must never know that I have been healing the boys.

I was working in my Bridge Hollow office when Gerry buzzed me. "One of your students is here to see you. Alexandra Doyle."

"Thanks. I'll come out."

Lexie was standing in the reception area by Gerry's desk. I got her a Snapple and led her back to my room.

"What can I do for you Lexie?"

"I saw on your website that you went to Vanderbilt University undergrad, and that you've done alumni interviews for them in the past."

"That's true." I smiled at her, and she relaxed in her chair. "Are you interested in Vandy?"

"Uh, actually, it's my top pick for colleges. Always has been." She giggled nervously. "It's kind of a joke around TA."

"Naturally, I applaud your decision. Vanderbilt's a terrific school. How can I help you?"

She swallowed. "I was wondering if you'd be willing to write me a recommendation letter."

"I'd be happy to do that for you, Lexie! But I'd rather not give them the same information that's already clear from your application. Let's schedule a mini interview in the next couple of days, so I can tell the panel about you—who you are as a person, what you enjoy, and why I think you'd fit in on campus. What's tomorrow morning like for you? How about an early breakfast at Nancy's Diner?"

We arranged to meet at seven. There was a pause.

"Ms. Carbury, you do trial work, right? You go to court?"

I made a face. "When I have to. Why?"

"This is hard for me, but I like the way...I mean, you handle the class really well. You don't put up with any, um...."

"Insolence? No, I do not." Was she going to tell me?

"And you're not a full time teacher, so they have no hold on you, right?"

"They? Meaning the Board; the Headmistress? No. I'm doing them a favor, in fact."

"So, you couldn't get into trouble with them?" In other words, whose side were you on?

"No Lexie," I said, as gently as I could. "I'm completely independent. There isn't anything that they could do to me. Nothing that would matter, anyway."

She sighed. "OK. Good. Then I have something to tell you."

If I hadn't already heard about the PETs from Carlie and Julie, I would have had trouble swallowing Lexie's story.

Since her freshman year at Tallmadge Academy, Lexie had been an innovator. An enthusiastic runner, when she found that TA did not have a girls' track team, she had convinced the BHS coach to let her compete with the boys. In her sophomore year she helped to persuade the TA Board of Directors to hire a coach for the girls. In Lexie's junior year she had been elected to Student Government, and had founded a project that taught studying skills to city kids in Hartford, Waterbury, and Torrington. Her committee had published a study aid booklet, which was now being distributed in public schools across the state. At the end of her junior year, Lexie had been elected SGA Social Chair.

That's when the trouble began, she explained.

"Every spring we wind up the school year with a big dance. The Social Chairs from TA and BHS work together—we pick the location, hire the band, choose a menu. It's like a huge wedding. The Social Committees come up with a list of three possible themes, and the two schools vote. Last year we did Knights of the Round Table—medieval costumes and food. We had kind of a King Arthur fair for the weekend." Lexie brightened for the first time. "It really came off well."

"What's this year's theme?"

"It's meant to coincide with the 250th anniversary of the founding of Bridge Hollow in 1762, so Colonial America, with an eye to the Revolution. We're going to set up a colonial village for the week—the town is doing most of that work; but there will be a parade, and lots of things to see and do. The dance will be held in the old ball room at the Morse Mansion in town."

"Sounds like fun," I grinned. "So? What started the drama?"

"I had an idea. Why not invite the other prep schools in the area? We compete with them at sports and academics, and they're rivals for college entrance stats. Let's have some fun with them for a change. I thought the multi-school dance would bolster camaraderie—all that good stuff."

"How did that go over?"

Lexie actually smiled. "Both sides of the river voted almost unanimously in favor of my proposal last spring, just as the final exam period started. The other academies were approached, and the responses were enthusiastic. The Social Committees met several times, and the thing was put into motion."

"And that's when the problem began."

"Yes." Lexie's face froze, and then began to crumple. "I honestly don't know how I got through finals, Ms. Carbury. The abusive emails, the crank calls—notes stuffed in my gym locker. At first I didn't know who was behind it, and then one day, Therese and about six of her cronies surrounded me when I came out of my French exam. They crushed me into a corner. They said I had no right to change the way things are at school. They told me to quit TA. They called me a…they said I was retarded."

"Why, for god's sake?" This was much worse than I had expected.

Lexie turned her head in shame. "I've been diagnosed with ADD, so I have permission to take more time on tests. It was never a problem before, and not a lot of people know about it. But since the whole thing with the dance…."

"The PETs decided to use it against you for more fire power." I could barely keep the rage out of my voice. "Did you tell any of the faculty about this?"

"Not then. I just went back home to St. Louis, and tried to have a nice summer. We had to keep working on the dance via email, of course, but the advisors see all of those—so nothing happened while I was away."

"Did you tell your parents?"

"No. I didn't want to worry them. They're so proud of me, and the tuition here is really expensive—like college. They've had to make a lot of sacrifices for me to go to TA. I wasn't eligible for financial aid. And I *really* want to get accepted to Vanderbilt. I have a much better chance with a TA diploma."

"But when your senior year began?"

"It's been horrible! The old stuff from last year started up again, but worse. Then I was getting mean texts on my cell. Sometimes with pictures. People giving me the finger; mooning me. Awful stuff on Facebook. Then the website went up, and it was all around all the schools that were invited to the dance."

"What website?"

She gave me the address. I walked over to my desk and brought it up.

Get Lexie!

Don't let that whoring bitch change our TA traditions! Sign your name to our petition, and we'll get her kicked out of school.

Close to one hundred names, female and male, were lined up in columns under the headline. These were interspersed with candid snaps of Lexie on different parts of the campus, and in town. The tame shots had her chewing, scratching an arm, or blowing her nose. The truly offensive photos were more intimate; including one of her backside as she bent over in running shorts, and several of her in profile in the gym shower. The worst showed her in semi undress with a tall blond boy. They were obviously engaged in sexual relations in a dorm room. Lexie's face was very clear—only the back of the boy's head was visible.

I had a flashback to my senior year at Vanderbilt. I was living in the sorority house, and my boyfriend at the time—Neil—had been almost a nightly visitor, a situation which broke rules and annoyed my housemates. I had been a college student of twenty-two. Lexie was still a minor in high school. I couldn't begin to imagine the devastation that she must have been feeling from this betrayal.

"I went to my dorm monitor in Barton Hall first. Gwen's a nursing student at a college in Massachusetts, just over the state line. She's really nice. She went to my Guidance Counselor with the story—I was too embarrassed. Mrs. Reynolds had a meeting with the Deputy Headmistress, Laurel Collier, who then had a meeting with my advisor, who is a History teacher here—Mrs. Furling. Finally, Yolanda Gibbs, the Headmistress, asked to see me."

"And what happened?"

"I got detention for having sex with my boyfriend in his room. The Headmaster of BHS was there for the meeting. They said I was lucky not to get expelled."

Lexie burst into tears.

After Lexie had washed her face and returned to class, I sat in my office staring out the window at the town green, until a knock at my door brought me back to earth.

"Do you want anything from the deli, Emma?" Valerie asked.

"Gerry's about to fax the office order." Valerie Richardson was one of the partners at Kilby and Richardson, from whom Denise and I rented my office space.

"Tuna on rye with lettuce and tomato. Ice tea with lemon," I replied. "Thanks Valerie." In a moment she was back.

"Was that one of your students?" She asked, taking a seat in front of my desk. "She looked pretty upset. She asked Gerry for some tissue. Is everything OK with your class?"

"Everything's fine," I replied, carefully. "One of the girls wanted to speak with me about an issue that is unrelated to academics."

"You do seem to get along well with these young women!" Valerie announced, getting up and going to the door. "Tallmadge Academy should put you on salary for counseling, as well as teaching."

"The girls know that I will be discreet," I replied coolly, picking up a file. "And that I understand the importance of boundaries in relationships."

CHAPTER NINE

Witchcraft

"Listen Carlie. I can't give you permission to take classes in witchcraft with me. I just don't have any legal authority to do that. You're still a minor. You have to ask your mom."

Carlie was disgusted. "Oh sure! The woman practically lives at church. Like she's really going to let me dance around circles and cast spells." Carlie dropped on to the arm of my club chair, pouting.

"I can't help that, honey. I'm sorry." I thought for a moment. "Although…."

She brightened. "A loophole?"

"You and Julie are buds, right? What if you went as Julie's guest? Nothing to do with me. If Sophie doesn't have a problem with it, you're in, and I'm off the hook."

Carlie pulled her cell out of her pocket, grinning. "Attorneys sure are tricky!"

"CYA is the name of the lawyer game, babe."

"Wiccans honor life," Sophie began. Eight students had fore-gathered in her witchcraft shop. "We live in the joy of the moment. We have a great reverence for nature, and animals. We honor the earth as sacred, and as the source of our magick. We are serious about ecology. We recycle, we compost, and we eat organic foods. Many of us are vegetarians. Wicca is a nature based religion. It is recognized by law, and protected as such by the U.S. Constitution. A case that was tried in federal court in Virginia in 1985 has validated Wicca in this country." She nodded to me.

"*Dettmer v. Landon*," I replied. "Affirmed in the United States Court of Appeals for the Fourth Circuit in 1986."

"Please understand that one does not have to be Wiccan to practice witchcraft. Magick is the ability to bring about change by moving energy. It is all around us, and within us. Tools such as wands, cauldrons, and athames help us to focus our energy, but they are not innately magickal. All that is required is your emotional concentration, and your intent.

"Wiccans do not have religious hierarchies, and they do not draw people to their religion, so our focus in these sessions will be on the practice of witchcraft. However, a brief history of Wicca should help you to understand where we are now, and how and why we got here.

"Originally, the word pagan referred to someone who lived in the country. Similarly, heathen meant one who dwelled on the heath. The Old Religion, which honored the God and Goddess, and gave reverence to the Earth, was still practiced in the country as Christianity grew and pushed it out of the towns. Eventually the term pagan was altered to mean one who was not a Christian.

"Ultimately, a clash developed between the evolving so-called medical profession, comprised of men, and the country herbalists and midwives, who were predominately women, and often the only healers available to the poor, and women in general. Much of their herb lore is still in use today. Fifteenth century physicians, who were reportedly less effective and more dangerous than female lay healers—consider the practice of bleeding with leeches—

decided to eliminate the competition. Then, as well as now, political and economic monopoly of the medical profession translated to control over the population; who will live, who is allowed to procreate, and who is considered sane.

"The medical men had the support of the Church, which viewed the empirical methods of wise women as a surrendering to the senses, and therefore a betrayal of faith. Fear was encouraged, as witchcraft was deemed to be practiced only by a follower of Satan. Legal proclamations were made, and witches were arrested and put to death. *The Malleus Maleficarum,* or *Hammer of Witches,* was written in 1486 by two monks, and for three hundred years was the handbook of witch hunters. Its directives subjected accused witches to various horrific tortures to force confessions and further accusations. In a calculated wave of terrorization created by the ruling classes, witches were burned at the stake, hanged, and crushed by heavy stones.

"By the late seventeenth century, surviving members of the Craft were practicing in secret, usually in tight knit family covens. Witches became so isolated from each other that they began to record spells, potions, and rituals in what became known as a Book of Shadows. It wasn't until the second half of the twentieth century that witchcraft was publically revived."

Sophie paused. "Before we move on, I want to be clear about an extremely important point. There is no such thing as Satan, or the devil, and the practice of witchcraft has nothing whatever to do with the concept of a horned evil being that supposedly makes bad witches do bad things. Are we clear?"

Everyone nodded vigorously.

"This brings me to the law of Karma. Can anyone tell me what that is?"

"The boomerang effect," one woman replied. "What goes around, comes around."

"In essence, that's correct. Witches observe what is known as the Threefold Law. Any energy we send out comes back to us, times three. If you say, or think, or do anything that is mean spirited, be advised! It will show up later in your life, in triplicate. The opposite is true as well, so make sure you spread the good stuff only. Karma is not a punishment. It is the Law of the Universe.

"Wiccans believe that we are all here to meet specific challenges and learn from them. Sometimes we are paying off a karmic debt from a past lifetime. And yes, we also believe in reincarnation, which provides an evolving soul a new classroom with every trip to this planet. Learning from past mistakes uncovers what might be inhibiting us from making progress in this life. So, take an honest look at how you're doing! I guarantee that if you've got a problem now, it's because you didn't take care of it the last time you were here. These issues reappear until you've learned your lesson, whatever that may be."

"Explains your lack of men," Carlie whispered. I felt like kicking her, but remembering the karmic return, I restrained myself.

Sophie moved to the center of the group. "OK! Who wants to learn about magick?"

"We all grew up reading *The Lord of the Rings*, right? And who here didn't cross her arms and blink, like *Jeannie*, or copy Samantha's nose wiggle from *Bewitched*? Later it was the *Star Wars* series, with its spooky Jedi knights, and light sabers that channeled the 'Force.' In the late nineties first *Buffy*, and then *Charmed*, hit Americans with the awesome power of beautiful young super witches who were saving the world every week. Finally, the *Harry Potter* books taught millions of people across the globe that good must always be victorious, even against the most terrible of monsters. Magick is everywhere, and it is present in all of us.

"Wiccans know that everything affects you, and you affect everything. We call this the 'ripple effect.' Imagine your energy moving away from you, like waves in the water. If you practice magick, you can truly change things, but with this power comes responsibility. Therefore the first question a witch asks before working a spell is 'How may I cause the least harm?' The Wiccan Rede, as it is called, is a simple eight word passage: *An it harm none, do what ye will.* Therefore, make sure that your magick hurts no one, not even yourself, before you begin.

"Wiccans follow a strong moral code. Being a witch means that you have committed to act for the greater good of the planet and its inhabitants, and that you will actively work to make the world a better place.

"The symbol of the Wiccan faith is the pentacle. It is a five pointed star with a single point at the top, and it is surrounded by a circle. The points represent the four elements, earth, air, fire and water, with spirit at the top. I'll explain the magick circle at our next class." Sophie looked angry for a moment. "There are many ignorant fools out there who believe that the pentacle is the symbol for satanic ritual. Once again, there is no devil in the Craft.

"Why do magick? All of you have probably heard the saying 'as above, so below.' The Universe is full of boundless energy, just waiting for you to tap into it. And you can use it at any time. Remember that magick utilizes energy to bring about a desired change. Perhaps you want to heal yourself, or someone else. Perhaps your life isn't moving along as smoothly as you like. Maybe you have a bad habit that you'd like to break, like smoking, or dating troubled partners. And of course, Love spells are numerous, and very popular. Magick will help you achieve your goals, and bring you closer to a feeling of wholeness. Everyone is connected."

Sophie looked around the room. We must have appeared a bit shell shocked.

"That's all for tonight, I think. Next time we'll discuss magickal tools, and tricks for enhancing your results. Feel free to look around the store. I'll keep it open for another half hour or so."

"Do you need anything?" I asked Carlie, who had immediately moved over to the jewelry counter.

"Need and Want are relative terms." She was fingering a blue and silver bracelet with three tiny pentacles. "Forty dollars. Ouch."

"Look, I can feel a manipulation coming on. If you really want it, consider it an early Christmas present. Just be careful where you wear it, OK? Tallmadge Academy is not exactly an open environment for earthy religions."

"Nope." Carlie agreed, putting the bracelet on her wrist. "Thanks, Emma."

"Pleasure. I remember being poor at your age. And I went to a wealthy kids' high school as well. No fun."

"What about you?" Carlie asked. "Anything you need?"

I steered her over to one of the windows, where an assortment of large glass balls were suspended at different heights with clear twine.

"Weird!" Carlie exclaimed, turning a green one in her hand. "There are finger thingies in there. What kind of ornament is this?"

"It's a Witch Ball," I replied, carefully removing a purple one from its hook, and reading from the attached card. "You hang them in your window to ward off bad spells. Legend claims that evil spirits are caught and held in the web like glass strands inside the sphere. Witch Balls were popular in England for centuries, and they came over to the colonies about the time of the Revolution. I've seen them at the Whaling Museum on Nantucket, but I thought they had something to do with fishing nets. I'm getting this one. It will be perfect in my bedroom."

Carlie sighed. "Yeah great. Maybe it'll warn you if you're about to sleep with a jerk."

CHAPTER TEN

Gymkhana

I met Tina Rosen at Gantry's in Fairfield Center.

"Great girl food here, huh?" Tina was enthusiastic about the menu. We both ordered cobb salads. "So you want to know about Arlene Pierce?"

"You were a clerk in Bridgeport at the same time that she was. Do you remember anything that would be useful in Judge Stevenson's defense?"

Tina leaned forward. "She was totally obsessed with the man."

"Arlene was assigned to Terry, right?"

"For a few months. Then the Chief Clerk, in her infinite wisdom, shuffled us all around. I ended up doing civil jury with Stevenson. Arlene got stuck with the Family Magistrate."

"How did Arlene react to this rearrangement?"

"She was livid. She was jealous that I got to spend time with the judge, and she didn't. She asked me a lot of questions about you."

"You mean about my dating Terry?"

"Yes."

"Did she say how she found out about us?"

"Judge Crockett blabbed."

"That old windbag!"

"Yeah, well everyone pretty much agrees he should be running a produce stand somewhere. As opposed to wearing a robe and making decisions about people's lives."

"How obsessed *was* she?"

"Remember how we used to have lunch with the judges in that big conference room?"

"The one with no windows? Sure."

"Arlene would scramble to get a seat next to him. Then she'd offer him items from her little brown bag. I think he was totally oblivious to what was going on. She would find excuses to run into his chambers, even when he was on the bench. It was weird. We all made fun of her."

"Did you ever go to any of the Bar Association functions?"

"A few. Arlene was always there if Stevenson went. Made sure she got a place at the judge's table."

"Did she ever say anything that could be useful?"

"I've been thinking about that since you called. There was one instance at the Christmas party that really stands out. Crockett put on a Santa suit and distributed the grab bag gifts. Stevenson's present was a how-to-be-romantic book, and a get-in-the-mood CD. He was horrified, and surreptitiously threw the entire package in the trash. Probably thought it was a joke from one of the other judges."

"He told me about that!"

"Well, what he didn't know was that Arlene was the one who got them for him."

"What makes you think so?"

"I was standing right next to her when it happened. There was a big crowd of us, but she started huffing and heaving—shoved her way out and headed for the ladies' room. I followed her. She was in a stall, crying. I heard her wail 'that son of a bitch' and 'I'm going to fix him.' It was creepy. I never let her know that I was in there."

"But isn't it absurd to suppose that she harbored this anger for years and is now trying to get Terry thrown off the bench?"

"Well, he married yet another clerk, didn't he? Fairly recently."

"That's true."

"He was sitting in Milford by then. Arlene must have kept tabs on him."

"Have you been contacted by the state investigator yet?"

"No, but it's only a matter of time."

"Will you do me a favor Tina, and let me know how it goes?"

"Absolutely. But you should talk to Julianne Meyer."

"The court reporter! She was friendly with Arlene, wasn't she?"

"She was. But there was some sort of falling out. Julianne might now be inclined to be helpful."

Julianne Meyer returned my call after lunch.

"Of course I remember you, Emma. You always had such beautiful suits."

"On a shoestring budget!" I recalled. "Tina suggested that I talk to you about Arlene Pierce."

"Now there's a woman who could do with some psychotherapy. The walking definition of self destruction."

"But you were friends with her at some point, weren't you?"

"Oh sure. But with the exception of her marriage, which is a whole other story, Arlene never stays in any relationship very long. Professional, or personal. I was lucky. Most of her victims end up at the wrong end of a lawsuit."

"Like Terry Stevenson."

"That poor man. But there never was a relationship there, as far as I could see. Not that Arlene didn't try real hard."

"What was your experience with her?"

"This happened about six months after you went into private practice. I had decided to resign from my court reporter position with the state and open my own business. Doing depositions and the like. Anyway, Arlene heard about it and approached me about renting office space in her family's commercial building in Stratford."

"Uh, oh."

"Exactly. First, there was no heat. Then, the plumbing problems. The parking lot was never plowed in the winter. I could go on. Naturally, I complained. I would get messages on my machine from Arlene that were so abusive, I was actually frightened. Then, the threatening letters started coming. Thank goodness, I had only taken a year lease. I moved my business to Milford, and I've been here ever since."

"Do you still have any of the tapes, or the letters?"

"Not the tapes, but I did keep some of the letters. She hand wrote them. For a lawyer, she wasn't very bright."

"Has the state investigator contacted you yet?"

"I'm scheduled for grilling next week."

"Would you mind making copies of those letters and sending them to me, before your interview?"

"Yes, of course. What's the matter? Are you worried that the State of Connecticut isn't going to do right by the good judge?"

"Something like that, yes. Those political turncoats in Hartford would think nothing of sacrificing a decent, hardworking man, just to get some good press for themselves."

October began with a beautiful Indian summer. The sky was cobalt blue, the foliage a glorious array of cadmiums and crimsons. The grass, reviving from the hot summer, returned to its splendid emerald shades.

Which in turn revived the horses.

"Are you sure about this, Joanne? Joy isn't exactly a group gathering kind of mare."

"She'll be fine. Just remember the basics, and don't ride over any of the ponies!"

Easier said than done. We were bracing ourselves for Apple Ridge's annual gymkhana. I was frankly concerned. I had never competed with Joy in any kind of event, and had only hacked her occasionally at various horse shows. This was going to be a challenge.

There were children on ponies everywhere. The staff had done a wonderful job of decorating the outdoor arena. There were cornstalks on all the jump standards, some with scarecrows, as well. Chrysanthemums and pumpkins were scattered around the ring, and several big tubs filled with apples in water were set at regular intervals.

The sign up sheet for the games was posted by the wash stall. The costume contest was first. After that, it was Simon Says, the Egg and Spoon event, and Sit-a-Buck. The tougher games were next. Red Light/Green Light, Bobbing for Apples, and Musical Barrels. I had entered the first four, feeling that any activity that involved multiple dismounting and mounting was not to be attempted. I could not imagine Joy standing idly by while I tried to bite a floating apple.

A little girl with a tiny gray pony clip clopped by. The pony was dressed as a ballerina, with sparkles in her mane and tail, pink tulle around her tummy, and pink ribbons laced up her legs. Her young owner had matching pink bows on the ends of her braids.

An older girl, probably in junior high, came in and proceeded to array her horse as a clown. He wore a big floppy hat, a white sheet with red pompons attached to it, red polo wraps on his legs, and face paint.

A third pony emerged as a cowboy, complete with Stetson and gun belt.

These animals really were terrific sports.

I had less praise for the parents. There is something about children in competition that brings out the worst in adults. Were they working off some aspect of frustration from their youth? Was the success of their offspring a validation of their existence on this planet? Or were they merely socially undeveloped, two dimensional jerks?

The results of the costume contest were as follows: the ballerina was first place, a pirate was second, and a zebra got third.

The youngest students began their division with an amusing game of Simon Says. I was aware that the adult riders were to perform last, after the teenage group, so I sat down and helped myself to some turkey chili from one of the tables.

A large, matronly female appeared to my right. She extended a beefy paw.

"I'm Mary Sue. That's my Christy on the pirate out there."

"She's a cute little rider."

"Thanks. She should be. She's at this barn every day."

"It's nice for girls to have a place to go and have fun."

"As long as it is fun, sure. I hear too many stories of kids throwing up before horse shows. It's a lot of money to spend to just be miserable."

"Joanne doesn't seem to be that kind of trainer."

"She's not. But others here are." I noticed Frank and Meredith drinking wine alone together in the gazebo. For a married woman, the owner of Apple Ridge Farm was certainly flirtatious. "A few of us are afraid that Jo will decide to go back into the big leagues again, now that her divorce is behind her."

I suppressed Mary Sue's obvious invitation to gossip. "I know how devastating the whole process can be."

"You're the lawyer, right?"

"Correct."

"Then, can you please explain to me why the judge gave my ex-husband joint custody of my kid?"

"I really couldn't say without studying the court's memorandum of decision."

"Here," she grunted, reaching into her bag.

I force fed myself the last of my chili and got up quickly. Why were people so clueless about social boundaries?

"I'm going to have to take a rain check on that. I still need to tack up my mare."

"OK, fine." Mary Sue turned to the barn mom on her other side. I made my escape.

Joy was busily licking her salt block. "Here I am Sweetie. Time to make you beautiful." She eyed me with suspicion, probably worried that I was going to whip out some pink glitter. I led her into one of the tack-up stalls. It had a Dutch door that opened out on to the festivities. Joy pushed her head through the window and surveyed the food tables. I got to one of the apple pies just seconds before she did.

I brushed out all the dust from the morning's rolling in the paddock. I applied shiny conditioner to her tail, and hoof polish to her feet. Her martingale, pad and saddle went on next. I took off my sneakers and pulled on my Vogel tall boots. Last, I detached Joy from the cross ties, took off her halter, and buckled on her show bridle.

When we got outside, the older girls were finishing up with Bobbing for Apples.

Melissa McCarthy had just dismounted and was fishing her chin around in the cold water. Her horse, a large chestnut named Caesar, was clearly tired of watching the humans grab all the apples. He glared at Melissa's upended posterior. He then swung his huge head down and bit it.

There was a yowl of pain.

We, the audience, were in an obvious dilemma. We felt sorry for the girl's distress. We were also in desperate need to laugh hysterically. Even the child's mother had a grin on her face. Joanne saved the situation by calling for the Musical Barrels participants to move into the ring.

Joy stood patiently while the prizes were handed out to the second division. Then, the adult class was instructed to mount up. I trotted Joy around the cornstalks, just to make sure that she was comfortable with their waving appendages. Then, I picked up a right lead canter. Except for some idle staring at the apple tubs, Joy was well behaved throughout the warm up.

One of the little girls provided me with an egg and a steel teaspoon. I held them balanced in my left hand and proceeded to circle at the walk with the other seven adults in the ring. We didn't lose anyone until the trot. Joy had very smooth gaits. Jaime on her big bouncy Wolfman, was not as lucky. By the time we were instructed to canter, we were down to three contestants. I decided to opt out of jumping cross rails and accepted third place. Jumping Joy with two hands was difficult enough.

Sit-a-Buck went well. The dollar bill flew out from under my leg over the first cross rail, and we came in fourth. Joy got jittery during Simon Says, and refused to come back to a walk from a canter, so once again we were in fourth place.

Then Joanne called for Red Light/Green Light to begin.

Never tell a big jumper to stop in the middle of a course. Joanne yelled "Red Light!" I said Whoa, and sat still in the saddle. Joy responded by standing straight up and bellowing at the gray gelding just in front of her.

I decided that Joy had performed her good girl quota for the day, dismounted, and led her back to the barn.

I collected our ribbons when the events were over, and we all moved to the tables for stew and wine. One of the mothers poured me a glass of chardonnay.

"Your mare looks like she's tough to handle," she remarked.

"She is. That's why I decided to quit when I did."

"Well, it's good that you know your limitations."

Oh good. Yet another competitive barn mom.

"Well done, Emma!" Joanne was beaming. "Joy behaved, and you looked like you were having fun."

"I have to admit to a streak of prize fever, though. Did you see me use my stick when she got jumpy during Sit-a-Buck?"

"Yes, but she listened to you."

"She was probably too shocked to do anything else. Joy's really not used to ponies."

"Especially not ponies in drag! But seriously, if you ever decide that you'd like to do a little C rated show with her, let me know. I've got a few adults who are ready to start with the small stuff, and you're one of them."

I felt sick to my stomach. "OK."

"You should be proud of yourself, Emma. Joy is a lot of work, and you practically learned to ride on her, as an adult. That takes a lot of guts. There isn't another amateur at this barn who could handle her." Joanne paused. "Not many professionals, either."

"Thanks, Joanne. That means a lot. It hasn't been easy."

"I can imagine. I've been teaching and training my whole life, but there have been plenty of times when I wondered why on earth I didn't just go to grad school, like my parents wanted."

"We have to do what makes us happy, I guess, and not waste time pleasing everyone else."

Joanne looked thoughtful. "Good to hear. I'll remember that the next time my mother starts her regular lecture."

CHAPTER ELEVEN

Familiars

Denise met me in my office when I returned from lunch. "Bad news, I'm afraid, Em. The Judicial Review Council found probable cause in Judge Stevenson's matter. A public trial has been scheduled."

"Do you know who testified at the hearing?"

Denise shook her head. "It was closed. But I was given some information from my friend on Stevenson's team. Arlene Pierce testified, of course. And her husband. There was a surprise witness, as well. A former clerk from Bridgeport. Apparently she declared that Pierce was not alone in the judge's attentions."

"Were you told the woman's name?"

"Not yet. But I'll squeeze it out of one of my sources, never fear."

"Because, without this woman, it would have just been Arlene's word against Terry's, and possibly no trial date."

"Exactly."

Tina Rosen was effervescent when she called that morning. "I've got dirt, Emma! You're going to love it!"

"Let me have it, honey!"

"She wrote a BOOK! Arlene Pierce wrote a book! All about some shrink she had twenty years ago and how he screwed her!"

"Literally screwed her?"

"Yes! They had a relationship. He left his wife for her. Then Arlene turned around and sued him."

"He deserved it," I replied, disgusted.

"Of course he did! The book is pretty graphic, Em. A friend of mine was a clerk in Bridgeport after Arlene left. She says that everyone was snickering about the sex scenes then. Even the judges."

"What's the title?"

"*Surviving Psychiatry*. The sad part is that Arlene admits that she was sexually abused by her father and has spent her entire life obsessing over and then destroying male authority figures."

"Like men in black robes, for instance?"

"Exactly. If Stevenson had been a normal lawyer, she probably never would have noticed him."

"Does anyone have a copy of this book?"

"I checked. It's out of print, but Amazon has a few used available, so I ordered a couple of copies. Should I send one to the Judicial Review Council?"

"Are you sure you want to get involved with the trial?"

"I could always send it anonymously."

"True. Hey Tina—do you have any idea who else could be accusing Terry Stevenson of inappropriate behavior?"

"Another clerk? They're coming out of the woodwork."

"Seems like it, doesn't it? We've heard through the grapevine that Arlene wasn't alone at that closed hearing."

"I'll ask around. I know people who work at the Attorney General's office. They hear everything."

Carlie was sitting in my library, doing her homework, when I got home that night.

"I put your bike in the garage, honey. Have you eaten?"

"I had meatloaf in the cafeteria," she replied. "I wanted to show you this." Carlie held up a new cell phone. "Mom and Dad sent it to me. They want to see videos of stuff I'm doing around school. Convenient, huh?"

I put my briefcase down by my desk and took off my heels. "I take it that this was your idea."

Carlie smirked. "Of course. Way easier to gather evidence on Therese and her wolf pack. It's no problem for me to keep an eye on them—half of them are at the boathouse six days a week. Oh!" She added, pulling a manila envelope from her backpack. "This is from Lexie Doyle. She said you wanted it."

Lexie had printed out every abusive email that she'd received since last spring. She'd also made copies of the various stages of the **Get Lexie!** website, and comments on various Facebook pages. She had provided me with a CD, as well as hard copies. My course on Evidence was certainly teaching her how to preserve a record.

"I'm putting these in my safe, along with your PETs photo, and anything else you recover." I went into the kitchen for a glass of wine. "I'm happy to see that Lexie trusts you, Carlie. I wonder how she made the connection."

"She said she'd seen us together on campus, and she'd read about the whole Mentee thing in the school paper. Lexie really likes you Emma. She says you're the one grown up she knows who has any guts."

"Sometimes I feel the same way," I said, a little tired. "OK, I'm going to finish my wine, eat something, change, and then we'll head over to Sophie and Julie's for class."

"As I said last time we met," Sophie began, "Magickal tools merely enhance our spell work. They are not inherently powerful. The energy comes from you."

She drew our attention to a table that had been placed in the middle of the room.

"We'll start with the most common items. The athame, with its double edged dull blade, usually has a black handle. It is meant to direct and cut energy, and is never used for anything else. For obvious reasons, an athame represents the God on your altar. The cauldron, on the other hand, represents the Goddess. It is used for holding ingredients or burning incense, and some witches fill it with water for scrying, which is a method of telling the future." Sophie said. She smiled. "Like Hermione Granger, I have zero patience with any form of divination. There's just too much room for error. So, if you want to learn about palm readings, crystal balls, or tea leaves, I encourage you to do the research on your own.

"A besom, or witch's broom, is used to clear energy for your magickal space." She held one up, lengthwise. "They were never mounted for travel, by the way, but there were, and still are, ceremonial uses. The idea that witches fly probably came from nervous Christians, who were secretly observing country people leaping brooms to manifest bountiful crops.

"A witch's journal is known as her Book of Shadows, and some witches keep a Grimoire, or recipe book as well, for potions. I have enough trouble remembering to augment my grocery list, so this is a one book household. Any questions so far?"

A young woman with red hair stood up. "I don't know about anyone else here, but I'm having a lot of trouble of dealing with all of this. I've attended the Methodist Church in town all of my life. Hearing about Goddesses and altars is making me feel very uncomfortable."

Sophie looked around the room. "Who else is struggling with these concepts?"

Most of the people in the room, including two men, raised their hands.

"This is a difficult issue for many of my students who are not pagan. The only thing I can say that might help is—be clear in your head about the feminine and masculine energies that surround us on this planet. Who or what you worship is personal to you. But try to imagine male birds, for example, without female birds. Or plants and trees without flowers or fruit. I believe that the biblical allegory of Noah's Ark was meant to teach us this lesson—the Earth will become healthy again only if there is a powerful balancing of male and female energies. Too much either way creates chaos."

"So we should think about nature in harmony, rather than organized religion," one of the men commented. "Thanks. That does clarify the problem."

"You've mentioned altars several times," another woman said. "I'm getting visuals of black candles, blood red wine, and creepy statues. Am I far off?"

There was a low murmur of private discussion. Carlie glanced at me quickly and rolled her eyes. Ignorance and fear. Always a deadly combination.

Sophie remained professional. "Perhaps this would be a good time to talk about covens and solitaires. Covens are groups of witches who practice magick, and conduct rituals together. There are vast differences in the various disciplines, and many covens create a unique combination to suit their needs. As I have said, there is no hierarchy, and witches do not proselytize.

"Therefore, your altar can be whatever you want it to be. I'm a solitary witch. I have never been a member of a coven, and the bulk of my knowledge has come from intensive research, and frankly, trial and error. I know what works best for me. For example, my altar, usually a large flat stone, holds a few of the store bought items that I've already shown you, and the rest are found in nature. Shells, stones, feathers. Flowers. I love candles, but never black.

And I often have my dog with me. She helps me feel grounded, and she's a powerful familiar."

"What's a familiar?" One of the women asked. "Isn't it always a black cat?"

"A familiar is a specific animal with whom you are close, who is here to help you learn a particular lesson. It may be a pet, or it may be a wild animal that spends a lot of time in your backyard. Animals are amazing teachers. For example, I know that Emma is unusually connected to her horse, and to her dog. Think about what each of these animals symbolizes. Horses are large and fast; very powerful beings. But as herbivores, they are vulnerable and often afraid—the term is spooked, I believe. They also have a history of centuries of control and mistreatment by humans. Dogs are associated with loyalty, protection, and unconditional love. They are regarded as 'man's best friend.'

"A power animal, in contrast, is the representative energy of a species. When you're doing magick you might want to tap into Bear, for example, for strength, or Hummingbird, for joy in the moment. Or Rabbit for fertility! Those of you who have done Shamanic journeying are already familiar with this concept.

"Let's talk about energetic clearing. There are many easy methods of preparing a space. You can use your broom—it needn't touch the floor. You can burn incense, or sprinkle salt water, or ring a bell. Feather fans work well. Also smudging with burning herbs, usually sage, but thyme and rosemary are also common. Some witches just visualize a cleansing breeze blowing out all negative energy. Whatever works for you. The same applies to your tools. Clear them with the most practical method. For example, you wouldn't dunk your athame in salt water, and you might prefer not to burn incense indoors. Always clear your tools before you use them, especially the first time. You don't want anyone else's energy interfering with your magick.

"Once your tools have been cleared, they need to be charged with positive energy. The simplest way to do this is to leave them in a window during a full moon, or in full midday sun. I invariably do one, or both of these things. I tend to follow the 'Keep it Simple' maxim with all aspects of my life, and especially with magick.

"Our next topic is Grounding and Shielding. Who here practices yoga?"

Most of us raised our hands.

"It is very important to ground yourself, before you do any spell work. What do I mean by grounding?"

"In essence you are anchoring yourself to the earth, for strength and protection," I replied. "Mountain pose works for me. Also, the lotus position."

"I lie flat on my back and breathe deeply," another woman said.

"Excellent," Sophie continued. "I stand up straight and visualize myself as a tree, with my roots burrowing deeply into the earth. How do you feel when you are grounded?"

"Peaceful," Julie said.

"Rock solid," one of the men added.

"In a bit of an altered state," I replied.

"Aha!" Sophie said. "Now we're getting warm. And when you're peaceful, rock solid, and in an altered state, what happens?"

"You're more aware," Carlie answered. "You're in tune. You're in the zone."

"That's called mindfulness, and it's when magick happens!" Sophie responded, triumphantly.

"I've felt that way in church," one of the younger women announced, clearly surprised. "The choir is singing, the candles are flickering. Sometimes there's incense. I check out a little, I guess. I'm there, but I'm not. Everything feels very safe and pleasant. Comfortable. Sometimes I'm so relaxed, I forget to pray. Is *that* what you mean by an altered state?"

"Definitely! Remember, all religions are shamanic in origin. And a shaman goes into an altered state of consciousness to conduct journeys and soul retrievals for clients. It's all the same, just with different labels and rituals attached.

"All right, so now you're grounded. But you need to protect yourself as well. Being open means just that. You are available to any energy that might come in, welcome or not. So you have to shield yourself. The simplest method—and again, I like to keep it simple—is to surround yourself with white light. You can use this form of energetic protection any time. It's especially effective in crowded, emotionally charged spaces, such as sports arenas, theaters, hospitals, or courthouses. I even use it before I go to the dentist—consider all the emotion flying around that office!

"Witches work spells with the intention to bring about a certain change, usually to themselves. At our next session we will discuss when and why Wiccans observe Esbats and Sabbats, and the rituals involved.

"For simple spells, you don't need a great deal of hoopla. Recall once more the Wiccan Rede—*An it harm none, do what ye will.* It is imperative that a witch is clear on her or his intent, and the possible consequences, before the spell is cast.

"A spell is a sequence of actions performed in order to manifest a witch's goal. You may also think of it as a recipe, or even a form of prayer. Note please the words *emotion,* and *intent.* These two elements are the core of any successful spell. As I have said many times, the Craft is all about energy. In spell work we are raising energy that will be directed toward our intent, and then released.

"There is usually a spoken element to a spell, often a rhyme. I'm awful at poetry, so I tend to just put in my request in basic prose. Say you need money to pay your fuel oil invoice. You may chant something along the lines of 'My heating bill is really high, send me the funds ASAP so I'll get by.' Light a green candle, visualize your checking account increasing to the desired amount, say your spell, and send the energy out."

"Why green?" Someone asked.

"Because it's the color of money," Carlie replied.

"You've been doing the reading!" Sophie exclaimed. "Well done. This brings me to my next point. Magick can be enhanced by a number of factors—colors, herbs, stones, flowers. Even days of the week, the time of day, the phases of the moon. The months of the year. In your hand-outs you'll see some basic tools to use. For example, money spells are bolstered if cast in the morning to mid-day, on Sundays or Thursdays, which are male energy days, and during a waxing to full moon. The magick is also more powerful with the use of herbs such as basil or bay. Jade and Peridot are powerful prosperity stones. Finally, Autumn is the best time of year to cast abundance spells. Think of squirrels collecting acorns for the winter. And ladies, believe it or not, menstrual cycles can make powerful magick, especially during a full, or new moon. Bearing all that in mind—any time is a good time to work magick!

"Are there questions? I realize that all of this is a lot to absorb."

Carlie raised her hand. "What is a poppet? They look like voo-doo dolls to me."

Sophie flipped to the back of the materials packet and held up a page. On it was the outline of what appeared to be a ginger bread man without a face.

"A poppet is a magickal doll, which Wiccans use for spells such as love, healing, or weight loss. They're supposed to be pretty powerful, although I have no personal experience. Again, you employ the color cloth that corresponds to your intent. Cut out two of these figures. Sew them together, leaving the head open. Then you stuff the poppet with herbs, flowers, stones—whatever you want to use. Magickal symbols or runes can be drawn or stitched onto the poppet. It is sewn up and kept in a safe place. To undo the spell—

say that you've lost the weight that you want—simply take the doll apart. I've recommended some resources for poppet magick."

"Wow!" One of the women exclaimed. "Much cheaper than what I've been doing. I'm going to give it a shot."

"Any last questions before we wrap up tonight?"

"What is So Mote It Be supposed to mean?" One of the men asked.

"It's said at the end of a spell; kind of a Wiccan version of Amen. Translations vary, but the most common one is: It is this way because I say so and it is my Will."

"Huh," Carlie said. "A little pushy, really. You're pretty much telling the Universe to get a move on."

"Works for me," I replied. "I want to feel that any spell I've cast is already doing its job."

CHAPTER TWELVE

Protection Spell

Saturday morning at six I presented myself at the boathouse for assignment to one of the women's boats. Art put me in a quad—after several weeks in the men's eight, this was a relief—with a CPA, a nurse, and a psychologist. I was walking down to the dock in my usual a.m. semi conscious fog, when Luke appeared next to me.

"We haven't scared you away, then," he said, grinning. "Good."

My knees suddenly turned to water, and I almost dropped an oar. "The early hour is a bit daunting, I admit," I said, hoping that my voice wasn't shaking. "But I love to row, and there isn't much time left to the season."

"As a member of the teaching staff, you're permitted to sign a boat out on your own," he said. "Did you know that?"

"No," I said, surprised.

"I keep my single here in the boathouse. If you'd like to row together some afternoon, I could arrange with the Coach to reserve you a shell. Are you interested?"

"I'm definitely interested," I replied, with feeling.

"How about Tuesday at five then? I'll meet you on the patio. My cell's in the alumni directory, if there's a scheduling problem."

The CPA was the self appointed captain of our quad. She

assigned herself the stroke position, placed the nurse at bow, with the therapist behind stroke.

The therapist, Prue, seemed nervous. She nearly damaged the boat several times on the ramp, and needed help getting her oars in the locks. I held the gunwale while she stepped into her seat and adjusted her shoes. I caught the CPA and the nurse exchanging eye rolls.

We pushed away from the dock and proceeded down the river toward the lake.

These women were not good rowers. Recalling my Westport Rowing Club days with Sam in our double, this experience was a little tame. Their timing together was less than impressive, and Prue, clearly ruffled, was always behind. At one point she banged her oar into the CPA. Stroke hollered 'weigh enough,' and we stopped dead, our blades feathered parallel to the water. The CPA turned in her seat, and growled at poor Prue. "Do you think you could follow along with the rest of us for a change? Look at Emma—her first time out, and she's got perfect timing. What the hell is the problem?"

Prue burst into tears.

We were out in the middle of Lake Washington, and it took nearly an hour to return to the dock.

I checked on Prue in the locker room. She was sitting on the bench, looking miserable. "How are you doing?" I asked.

"Not so good," she said. "Those women are just awful—I don't know why I put up with it."

"Why *do* you put up with it?" I wanted to know, sitting down next to her. "This isn't high school gym class. You don't have to be here."

Prue blew into her tissue. "Oh yes I do! My husband is Will—on the men's team. Both our kids row here. My dad rowed here as a boy. It's expected."

Were her children named Muffy and Skip for god's sake? Was she about to change into a twin set and pearls? "Listen, you're the psychotherapist. We're strangers, so feel free to tell me to take a hike—but that's just nuts. These people can't make you row if it isn't your gig. What do you *want* to do?"

"I like skating. I want to skate." She sniffed again, and picked up her bag. "I used to do competitions as a girl, and I really enjoy playing hockey."

"Well, I happen to know that a women's hockey league practices at the BHS rink. I think they're called the She Lions."

Prue smiled. "You have a point. I've paid my dues. Now I want to have some fun."

"What about your rowing date with Luke?" Angela asked.

I felt my face turn red. "What about it?"

"How did it go?"

"It was very pleasant. We had good weather for it, and the kids were off the water by the time we started. He didn't shoot ahead of me, which was kind. We did a nice, easy loop around the lake, and came in."

"That was it? What did you talk about?"

"It's kind of hard to talk and row if you're not in the same shell, Angela. It's a pretty active sport."

Angela sighed. "Did you do anything afterward?"

"It was close to six thirty by the time we were done. We both needed to get going." I thought for a moment. "I did tell him that I was done with the Masters nonsense, although I didn't put it like that. I've never wanted to compete. He agreed that he preferred to go out in his single as well. So we're going to continue once or twice a week until the season's over."

"Well, it's something anyway," Angela said.

"What did you hope would happen, Ange?" I asked, annoyed.

"Did you want us to pull up on one of the islands, rip off our high visibility gear, and get down to it? I just met the guy. I don't know a thing about him. No one does."

Angela was apologetic. "You're right, Em. I'll back off."

I took a deep breath. "No, please don't. You're one of the few people I trust implicitly. I really want Luke to be another. He's obviously interested, and he's taking this very slowly and carefully, which I really appreciate. But how do I know? How can I tell what kind of man he is? What if he is really another Nick in disguise?"

"Then it's a damn good disguise, you have to admit, right? Did Nick start out this way? If I recall, he bowled you over with his judge's almighty-ness, immediately took you on a weekend in Maine somewhere, practically forced you to have sex with him, and then asked you to hold money for him so his ex wife wouldn't find out about it."

"Good point."

"That was nearly fifteen years ago, remember. You're a lot older and wiser now, Emma."

"Thanks."

"Just trust your gut. Isn't that what you're always telling me?

That night I fell asleep in front of the fire.

I am working a protection spell for Zachary. I take a large square of blue cotton and sew it carefully into a pouch. I fill it with herbs that I have charged in the full moon—lavender, mint, thyme, rue, rosemary, balm and basil. I light a candle, and I chant a rhyme for his safety.

Gods and Goddesses of War, Powerful Ones
Ares, Mars, Athena, Minerva, and Sun
Grant Zachary your Protection, your Skill, and your Might
Please guard him as he joins the Fight

I release my intention into the flame, and watch it soar upward into heaven.

I hurry to the stable, and soon Merry and I are galloping into town. Zack is alone in his chambers. He is packing his books and papers into trunks.

"Hannah, what are you thinking?" He hurries to the window. "Were you seen?"

"I left Merry with the blacksmith," I assure him, pulling down my hood, "and came through the alleys. We are safe."

I walk toward him with the talisman. I place the long cord around his neck, and tuck the pouch inside his shirt. "Promise me that you will always wear it. Tis strong magick." I move both my hands to his chest, and look up at his face. There is love there, but something else. Anger? Or dismay?

"Tell me Zack. If I had agreed to come with you to Boston—if I had decided to leave Joshua and a respectable life. Would you be on your way to fight now?"

He nods. "I have to do what is right. You know that. You understand me, Hannah."

"Always." I smile. "This may be our last chance to say farewell." I blow out the only candle. Taking his hand, I gently draw him toward the empty room in back.

Carlie, Lexie, and Julie were sitting in my Bridge Hollow office. I joined them at the small conference table in the corner.

"We have information, Emma," Carlie reported. "And we have some new recruits."

"Heather and Jeanne from class," Lexie added, "and a few of the younger rowers."

"Excellent!" I grinned, suddenly seeing us as a secret meeting of 'Emma's Spies.'

"The news is partly about me," Julie said. "I'm a target now."

This was inevitable. "I'm so sorry, Julie. But I'm not surprised. You're a scholarship student with a single mom. Do they know about the witchcraft?"

"Yep," Carlie replied. "They saw the pentacle on her bracelet. You were right about being careful, Emma."

"They know about my mother's classes, her shop—everything. They're saying that I have no real dad—that I'm some kind of devil's spawn. There's all kinds of crazy stuff on Facebook. I'm getting emails and texts every day."

"Here are the emails," Carlie said, pulling her backpack toward her. "And I took photos of the texts. We have the cell numbers too."

"And Therese painted a red gallows on my locker," Julie continued.

"How do you know that Therese did the artwork?"

"Carlie took a movie of her doing it."

"Here," Carlie said, rummaging in her bag, "I downloaded it for you."

"Amazing Carlie! What about you, Lexie?"

"I'm practically living with Gwen now—the dorm monitor. My roommate won't speak to me. Yesterday, when I got back from class, there was a FOR RENT sign on my bed. She'd dumped all my books and stuff in a pile in the middle of the room."

"Here's the photo," Carlie added. What else did she have in that bag?

"Gwen has tried a couple of times to talk to the Deputy Headmistress. She sends emails and real letters, but she keeps getting blown off."

I held my hand out. Carlie produced a folder.

"What about your advisor?"

"Mrs. Furling says I need to toughen up. She says that if there's any physical violence, she'll go to the Headmistress again."

"Great."

"My boyfriend dumped me," Lexie reported, sadly. "He said that he really likes me, but he just can't handle the drama."

Another casualty.

"Ladies, I'm no computer genius—but is there any way we can track these emails? What about the **Get Lexie!** website?"

"It's tough," Carlie said. "They can have a hundred screen names. But I have a plan. I've decided to become one of Therese's gang—you know—get inside the enemy camp. Our rowing team is kicking ass, and Therese keeps telling me that I've made a big difference at the races. She loves me. I'll start hanging out with her crowd. That way I can get real evidence of what's going on."

I was terrified. "You mean you'll become a mole? Carlie, these girls are really nasty pieces of work. What if you get hurt?" What would her mother do to me?

"But you can't stop me right? You don't have the authority?"

Attagirl! "No, I do not." Query whether I had a duty to inform her parents, however.

"Heather and Jeanne are gathering information from the track team," Lexie said. "Julie and I aren't the only victims in the school."

"Yeah," Carlie added. "Therese likes variety when she tortures kids."

Tina met me for lunch on Monday, a triumphant smirk on her visage.

"Phoebe Klein! She was the mystery clerk, Em!"

"That skinny, nondescript bird! How did you find out?"

"I used to date a guy in the Attorney General's office, who knows the investigator that the Judicial Review people use."

"Did you hear about her testimony?" We both glanced around the room. No one within eavesdropping range.

"She complained that Judge Stevenson made inappropriate comments to her."

"Were there any witnesses produced?"

"Nope. Phoebe also said that he would come up with reasons to get her in his chambers alone, and that he would call her at her desk in the clerk's office constantly, and send her notes."

"Any of these notes entered into evidence during the hearing?"

"Apparently not. Pretty lame, huh?"

"Pathetic. I can't believe they found probable cause based on this nonsense. I used to clerk for Terry. He called me at my desk and left notes in my box constantly, too. But it was always case related. The man is a machine. One of the hardest working judges on the bench. This is a disgrace."

"Here's Phoebe's email and phone number. She's working for one of the big firms in Hartford now, doing insurance defense litigation. What do you want to do?"

"Arrange a meeting. I know she's lying. I want to find out why."

"You think that the threatening postcard you got last week has something to do with this, don't you?"

"Of course. It's suspiciously similar to the notes that were sent to Julianne Meyer, who was having landlord tenant problems with Arlene's family. Somehow Arlene has heard that I'm asking questions. Maybe the state investigator tipped her off. Curious that my involvement worries her."

"Maybe part of it is jealousy. Stevenson was never interested in her, after all. I sent a copy of her book to the JRC attorney, by the way. Anonymously. I even wore gloves and used a sponge to seal the envelope. I felt like an ass doing it, but it's for a good cause."

"The State seems all too ready to hang Stevenson by his toenails. Sanctimonious pricks! I wish there was some way we could blast them without doing harm to Terry's career."

Tina attacked her crab cakes with gusto. "Not while he's a judge, anyway. He could always write his memoirs later."

Denise called me that evening. "I have an idea, Em. I tried a slip and fall case against Phoebe Klein a few years ago. We ended up settling before the case went to the jury, and she and I became friendly. What if I ask her out to lunch, and you show up?"

"Perfect! Thanks Denise."

"No problem. I made such a mess of things in the beginning, I feel like I owe you over this one."

Annie was in my office when I walked in. "There's a voice mail message that you should hear, Em," she said, an odd expression on her face. She pressed the Play button. "LISTEN BITCH. YOU AND YOUR FRIENDS HAD BETTER KEEP YOUR NOSES OUT OF MY BUSINESS! BUTT OUT!"

"She appears to be fond of anatomical references," Annie remarked.

"Arlene again. Can you save this for me Annie?"

"Sure. Have you and Denise set up a lunch meeting with the former clerk who testified against Stevenson?"

"Phoebe Klein. Yes. Wednesday at one in Farmington."

CHAPTER THIRTEEN

Drawing Down
the Moon

"Since this is our last session in this series," Sophie began, "I'm going to demonstrate a magick circle. Anyone who wants to participate may join me. All the others may take chairs outside the circle and watch.

"Tonight is a full moon, and the sun has set, so we are better able to tap into the moon's energy. It is also a Friday, which is associated with the goddess Venus, so a great time for spells having to do with love and healing. Remember, however, that you can do magick whenever you want. The time of day, phases of the moon, et cetera will merely make your magick stronger.

"A few words about Esbats and Sabbats first. An Esbat is a Moon ritual, honoring the Goddess, which is celebrated at night, during any phase of the moon. You can participate in as many Esbats in a month as you choose. We are holding one tonight.

"Sabbats are Wiccan holidays which honor the Sun, or male God. Recall that Wicca is a Nature based religion. There are eight Sabbats. They celebrate the Equinoxes and the Soltices, known as the Lesser Sabbats, and the mid points between the four quarters of the year, known as the Greater Sabbats. These last four mark the turning of the seasons.

"As we are here to learn about witchcraft, and not Wicca as a religion, I will leave it to you to research the Wiccan calendar and its holidays if you so choose."

"Is Halloween a Sabbat?" One man asked.

"We call it Samhain. It is considered the Wiccan New Year, and is probably our most important spiritual event."

"What about Christmas?"

"Yule, one of the Lesser Sabbats, is celebrated on the Winter Solstice, which is the longest night of the year—usually December 21st. We celebrate the rebirth of God, and participate in much of the same rituals as Christians do, including gift giving, singing, decorating trees, and mistletoe. And of course, burning the Yule log.

"All right! Back to the Moon and its energy. Have any of you ever noticed that things get crazy at the time of a full moon? Fights, accidents, lots of babies born? Your animals act a little whacky? That's because the energy of the moon is at its peak. As a witch, I do most of my magick during a full moon. I feel that my spells get that extra punch, and things move much quicker. When you're a person who likes action, as I do, this is particularly gratifying.

"Does anyone here know what a waxing moon is?"

"The moon is starting to show itself again after a new, or dark moon," Carlie replied.

"Exactly. In the sky it looks like a backwards capital C. Many witches utilize this energy to start projects, or bring new things into their lives. OK, so what's a waning moon?"

"The opposite," one of the women said. "The lunar cycle is almost over, and the moon is starting to disappear in the sky. It looks like a capital C."

"Perfect. The waning moon is a good time to banish bad habits, like smoking, or that job that you've been meaning to quit. So, if you want to learn the Wiccan symbol for the phases of the moon, it's the backward C, then a capital O, then a C facing the correct way."

"What about the new moon?" Someone asked. "What kind of magick should you do then?"

"Many witches suspend spell work when the moon is dark in the sky," Sophie explained. "It's supposed to be a low energy time." She looked out the window. "It looks as though we're all set outside. Will you please leave your watches and cell phones on this table, and step this way?"

Sophie opened the French doors and led us out into her back yard, a huge field bordered with maples, a few birches, and some enormous old oaks. The front portion of the field had been mowed, and before us was laid out a large circle in votive candles. In the middle of the ring stood a huge boulder, with another flat stone on top.

"I had Julie light the candles while we were inside talking," Sophie explained. She indicated folding chairs lined up against the back of the store. "Any viewers, please take a seat. Ground—as I have taught you, wrap yourselves in white light, and be as silent as you can. The rest of you follow me."

Besides myself, Carlie and Julie, two of the women had decided to participate. We walked through the flickering circle and stood with Sophie by the altar. There were several items sitting on a pink cloth on the flat surface—my small black cauldron filled with smoldering rose incense; some rose quartz, two scallop shells, one contained salt, the other water; my black handled athame, more candles and a small snuffer. The largest candle, pink, was in the middle of the altar, standing unlit on a silver pentacle. A drum, much like mine, was leaning against the stone. My Book of

Shadows was open, and marked with a pink rose. Sprigs of lavender and rosemary were tied together with a pink ribbon.

"This circle is nine feet from the altar in each direction," Sophie told us. "The space has already been cleared of negative energy with the incense. Recall that roses are the most powerful of the flowers for summoning love and romance. The herb bundles here are also strong energy for love spells. All of these tools have been cleared and charged.

"The four elements are represented. Earth in the pentacle and the salt. Air with the incense and the athame. Fire and water. According to myth, Venus, or Aphrodite as she was known to the Greeks, arose from sea foam on a shell. I have therefore included two scallop shells on our altar. Each item has been placed with their corresponding directions, or Quarters in mind. Earth at the North. Fire at the South. Water at the West, and Air at the East. The God and Goddess are represented here in the form of the ritual knife and cauldron. The yellow candle is for the God, the white for the Goddess.

"Take note that some of us are wearing pink tonight. Colors enhance the power of a spell or ritual. Many witches have ceremonial robes, but I tend to stay with natural fibers such as cotton, linen, or wool.

"As I have said, magick is about raising energy and then releasing it. Think about college sporting events—pep rallies, cheerleaders, bands marching, Homecomings for the alums. Everyone wearing the school colors and shaking pennants. Stadium waves. The goal is to create an emotional frenzy among the spectators and team members. This buoys up the players, and everyone shares in the positive atmosphere that is generated. Consider rock concerts, or musical theater that encourages dancing in the aisles. The concept is exactly the same.

"I ask that you all ground yourselves now. Stamp your feet

three times, and visualize tree roots dropping from your ankles and anchoring your bodies to the earth. Breathe slowly and deeply." Sophie looked at me. "Emma will be conducting this ceremony. I will be assisting. She has created a list of qualities that she desires in a man. She is asking the Universe to send her a true love."

Carlie squeezed my arm. I gulped. I hadn't been this nervous since my first appearance in court, nearly twenty years before.

I picked up my athame and walked to the edge of the circle that faced North. Stretching my right arm straight in front of me with the blade flat and pointed out, I began to walk slowly around the ring.

"No one has touched Emma's knife, or any of the items on the rock. Emma came early and set this altar herself. She is now casting the magick circle, moving what is known as deosil, or in the clockwise direction. She will do this three times. A magick circle is actually a sphere, or bubble of energy around, above, and below us. The circle is creating a between-the-worlds space, where we can work spells, and connect safely with other entities. It will contain any energy that we build up, until we release it. Once the ring is in place, you may only walk outside it if you cut a doorway with your athame. Animals, however, may move in and out at will. As she walks, Emma is focusing on her goal. She is visualizing pulling up a circle."

I moved back to the altar and took my place in the middle, facing North. Sophie smiled at me and nodded. I looked down at my Book of Shadows and read out loud.

Into our circle I invite the Four Quarters
North, East, South and West
And the Four Elements
Earth, Air, Fire and Water
Goddess and God, please enter our circle

And empower our magick
Tonight and for always
So mote it be

The moon suddenly appeared as a cloud moved west. We all looked up. Sophie held her arms over her head and laughed. I felt a tingle that started at the top of my head and ran down through my entire body until it disappeared into the earth. Every woman in the group appeared mesmerized by the power of the moon's energy. The sensation of connection to the Universe was intense. Carlie's eyes were wide open in amazement.

"Focus on your intent, Emma," Sophie whispered. "Really feel this man, this love of your life, as though he was standing right here with you. Embrace the emotion. Ask the Universe for what you seek."

I bent over my Book again and read out loud.

Please help summon the perfect love to me
When the timing is right
As I desire
So mote it be

I read through my list of qualities, my intent clear and strong. Sophie picked up her drum and began beating a slow, deliberate one, two, three, four rhythm. She started at the North, and walked around us, staying within the circle of lights.

"Now we can build up the Cone of Power with our energy," she announced. "Everyone follow me. As the drum beat gets faster, so will our pace."

We did as she said, and as the walking progressed to nearly running, I felt a change. The energy within the circle was mounting, and the atmosphere around us was heating up. The six of us jogged with the beat of the drum until it seemed that the air was too heavy to breathe.

"Now Emma!"

I ignited my list with one of the candles and watched it curl and burn on the stone.

"Everyone visualize the energy moving up and out of the circle, like a funnel or cone. Send it up into the Universe!"

I lit the pink candle in the center of the altar.

My soul mate is in this flame I see
Please send my wish, my dream love to me

The ladies all gathered around me. Sophie gave thanks to the Elements, the Directions, and to the Deities. "Farewell," she said.

I picked up my athame and faced North, walking in the opposite direction.

"Emma is now taking down the magick circle. She is moving widdershins, or counterclockwise, three times around the ring. The rest of you, please ground again. Send all excess energy back to the earth."

Finally, I snuffed the pink candle. "So mote it be," I whispered.

Carlie and I stopped at the Coffee Common for two chai lattes.

"So that was Drawing Down the Moon," Carlie mused, spooning some foam into her mouth.

"I beg your pardon?" I asked, still a little foggy.

"Honestly, Emma," she scoffed, "don't you read your own books? Drawing Down the Moon is a full moon ritual. It's performed during Esbats. You saw Sophie—she was pulling the Goddess energy into herself through her arms. You're supposed to visualize the moon's light flowing into you—recharging you. You felt that, right? I sure did."

"So that explains all the tingling!" I said amazed. "I was so focused on my spell—everything else was a blur."

"Your spell was seamless," Carlie assured me, taking a bite of biscotti. "Very powerful, and feminine and romantic at the same time. Like you. If that doesn't bring in your dream man, I don't know what will."

CHAPTER FOURTEEN

Luke

As I walked into my Bridge Hollow office the following Tuesday, Gerry buzzed. "There's a Luke MacLaren holding for you, Emma. Shall I connect him?"

I experienced a swooping sensation in my solar plexus, and then something that felt like a fountain shot up into my chest. "Please."

"Emma!" Luke's deep voice came through. "I hope this is a good time. I was wondering if you were free Saturday evening. One of my clients is opening his new French bistro—there will be wine tasting, and music. Would you care to join me?"

Oh thank you Universe!

I remembered to soften my lawyer's voice to regular volume. "I'd be delighted, Luke. You've made my day," I added, truthfully.

"Good! I'll be at your house at six thirty."

Denise called me early on Wednesday. "OK, here's the plan," she said. "Phoebe is meeting me at Alberto's at one o'clock. You'll wait in your car until you see her go in. She drives a blue Toyota SUV. Give us about ten minutes and then walk in casually. I'll pretend to suddenly notice you and wave you over."

"Sounds good. I'm not much of an actress, though."

"Don't worry, just follow my lead. Something's going on here, and we're going to pull it out of her." She paused. "Maybe I'll order a pitcher of margaritas with lunch."

I parked my Audi directly across from the entrance to Alberto's at precisely ten to one. Denise was just pulling up in her silver Lexus. She looked in my direction, but didn't wave, and proceeded into the restaurant. I began to feel a little ridiculous. All I lacked was a secret decoder ring and a camera in my powder compact.

At one o'clock, I spotted Phoebe. She was still a walking string bean, with limp, dull red hair, freckles, and fat lips. She was wearing a pink coat dress and beige heels, and swinging a black leather shoulder bag. An uncoordinated flamingo with accessory issues.

I listened to the radio for a few minutes and then made my scheduled appearance.

Denise had positioned herself in a corner away from the windows and had placed Phoebe with her back to the room. Denise waited until I was practically upon them before she feigned recognition.

"Emma! I didn't realize that you'd be in this area today. Are you alone?" She was already pulling out a chair. Phoebe swung her long neck around. She was clearly rattled.

"Yes. Thanks." I duly sat.

"Do you know Phoebe?"

"Only by sight. How are you?"

"Good," she stammered. "I'm good."

The waitress had excellent timing. "Have you decided?"

"A Rueben platter, please," Denise said promptly.

"Just onion soup for me," Phoebe said.

"Turkey club, please. Rye toast and an ice tea with lemon."

The waitress removed herself. Denise leaned forward, a cold

smile on her face. "Emma and I are law partners, you know Phoebe. We go way back. We were classmates in law school before she clerked in Bridgeport Superior Court."

"Uh, actually, I didn't know that."

"Oh yes," Denise replied. "Way back. And seeing as we are all former clerks here today, I was just wondering. What exactly is it that Arlene Pierce has on you? What would induce a Connecticut attorney to lie under oath to the Judicial Review Council?"

Phoebe's pink beak hung open. She emitted a squawk. "How did you know?" She whispered. "Who told you?"

I felt a wave of compassion. "Just fill in the blanks for us, Phoebe, and we'll take care of Arlene. She won't bother you anymore."

Phoebe took a big gulp from her water glass. "It was a few months after you left the clerk's office, Emma. Arlene *really* doesn't like you. Anyway, I was having terrible problems with money. You know how bad the pay was. One morning, I was flat broke. Nothing in my checking account; my credit cards were maxed out. My gas tank was empty. I couldn't even buy lunch. And then, I opened a letter from a *pro se* divorce defendant. He was requesting several certificates of dissolution, and he had enclosed a twenty dollar bill. Well, I mailed him the documents, but without a receipt. I never processed the cash into the computer. I put it into my wallet, instead." She sighed. "I guess Arlene must have been watching me."

Denise looked as sad as I felt. We both remembered those very lean days.

"When did Arlene approach you about this?" Denise asked quietly.

"Not for several months. She asked me to cover for her so she could take off early one afternoon. I told her that I wouldn't lie for her, and that's when she let me have it. She threatened to get me fired. Worse, she threatened to report me to Statewide Grievance and have me disbarred. I kept thinking of the thousands that I still owed in student loans, so I gave in."

"Since then, how often have you had to cover for Arlene, Phoebe?" I asked.

"Two more times while I was still working for the State. Then, I got that first job doing insurance defense. I thought I would be free of her, finally. But she emailed me a few weeks after I started, saying that she would tell my new bosses."

"Do you still have the note?" Denise looked excited.

"Yes, in my desk at home. I'll send you a copy of all her emails."

"What did she want you to do for her? You couldn't cover for her at the courthouse anymore."

"Legal research. I can't tell you how many briefs and motions that I've ghost written for her over the years. And now this poor judge."

"Arlene wanted you to fabricate a harassment charge against Terrence Stevenson?" I asked.

"So you committed perjury at his probable cause hearing," Denise added.

"Yes," Phoebe admitted, miserable. "I've been such an unbelievable fool."

"No, you've been the victim of a bully, and a blackmailer," Denise replied. "I'm going to fix this for you. I'll have a discussion with the attorney for Judicial Review."

"What will happen to me?" Phoebe panicked.

"We'll cut a deal with him. Thankfully, Judge Stevenson's hearing was closed, so the press knows nothing. Leave it to us. We'll take care of the matter of Arlene Pierce."

Our lunches arrived. Phoebe had three sips of her soup, put some money in the middle of the table, excused herself, and hurried back to her office.

"That poor woman," Denise said, chewing an onion ring.

"And that vicious, twisted bitch," I responded. "Well, this will get Terry off the hook. Thanks Denise."

"Any time. I never could stand Arlene."

"What are you going to wear tonight Em?" Angela asked. "Something smashing, I hope."

"I was thinking of my dark green wool dress with the scoop neck and long sleeves—maybe with an Hermès scarf, and pearls."

"Sophisticated, elegant, and sexy," Angela approved. "Very French. Heels?"

"But of course! Luke is six three. He can handle it."

"What does this wonder man look like? You've hardly said. All I know about him is that he's a landscape architect, he has a family farm up your way, and he rows."

"You know as much as I do Ange! Carlie says that Luke looks a lot like Timothy Dalton, back in his James Bond days."

"Wow! Then he's hot! Not the accent though?"

"Nope, although Luke's family is originally from the British Isles. Highland Scots. MacLaren—I looked it up."

"Didn't Dalton play Mr. Rochester in *Jane Eyre?*"

"Oh yes," I replied, a little embarrassed. "My favorite rendition, actually. I have the DVD—watch it every Christmas."

Angela chuckled. "You've been wild about Rochester since honors Lit our junior year. I remember how moony you got over him in class."

"It's a lot more fun to moon over the real thing—trust me."

Luke arrived in his Range Rover promptly at six thirty. I introduced him to Abby, who wagged her tail, and was immediately flirtatious.

"Sorry about the truck," he said, giving me a hand, "but my car is at the dealership."

"Not to worry," I replied. "Horsewomen are hardy specimens."

We were silent for a bit. I felt as though every nerve in my body was awake and wired. It was marvelous.

"Tell me about your horse," Luke said. "I've seen the pictures on your website. What's her name?"

"Ballygowan Joy. Joy for short. She was born on a breeding farm in County Kilkenny, Ireland—comes from a long line of super jumpers over there."

"Do you show her?"

"I've had her shown by professionals in the past. I'm concentrating on *my* riding now. What about you?" I asked. "Do you ride?"

"All my life," he said, grinning. "But nothing fancy. I keep a few saddle horses in the barn—they share quarters with the goats. I travel a good deal for work," he added, "so I have a couple who live on the grounds and take care of the animals for me."

The drive was about fifteen minutes. Café Auguste was located on the river, with an outdoor patio and white lights twinkling from the trees. The garden was beautifully laid out, with a nod to every season.

"Did you design this?" I asked, amazed.

"Do you like it? The owners wanted the view to the river to be spectacular, regardless of the time of year. Difficult to achieve in northwest Connecticut! But I'm pleased with the result."

We were seated in a quiet corner at the back. The entire wall was glass, and the view of the river was lit by spotlights. A small waterfall was directly in front of us.

We ordered chardonnay for the first part of the wine tasting.

"You're a fascinating woman," Luke said, after we had ordered.

"Why?" The owner had sent us a complementary cheese plate. I picked up a wedge of camembert.

"There are many reasons. Not the least of which is the fact that you don't ask questions. As a trial lawyer, you must be brilliant at cross examination."

I laughed. "Only when I'm on duty, I assure you."

He didn't reply.

"I don't ask questions for the simple reason that I don't like answering them," I explained. "I come from a nosy clan of intrusively inquisitive people. It's a sore spot with me."

Luke nodded. "I can appreciate that. On the other hand, I would really like to get to know you better."

"Tell you what—I'll start the ball rolling," I said, a mock serious tone in my voice. "Let's begin with the obvious. Mr. MacLaren— are you single in the legal sense of the word? Rather than the merely emotional?"

"Yes."

"Are you capable of understanding—and observing—healthy boundaries in a relationship?"

"I believe so. Yes."

"Are you attracted to women, as opposed to men?"

"Definitely."

"Now here's the big question. Are you suffering from any form of insanity, including—but not limited to—manic depression, paranoid schizophrenia, or some level of personality disorder?"

He considered this. "Not that I'm aware of."

"Excellent," I said, picking up another piece of cheese. "That's all I need to know."

Our appetizers arrived with more wine. I dove into my arugula and endive with goat cheese. I loved walnuts in a salad.

Luke was impressed. "An enthusiastic appetite. I'll add it to my list."

"Wait until the main course comes!" I laughed, dipping some bread into olive oil.

"Is it my turn, Emma? May I make a few inquiries?"

"Of course."

"I take it that you are single as well?"

"In every sense of the word."

"Have you ever been married?"

"Yes."

There was a pause. "But you don't want to talk about it?"

I put down my fork. "I just don't believe in stirring up the past, Luke. What's done is done. We can learn from our mistakes, naturally. I feel that they should be addressed properly, and then cleared out. But bringing up old drama again and again is—in my opinion—completely useless."

"You don't believe in psychotherapy?"

I rolled my eyes. "Don't get me started."

Luke appeared to be weighing his next question carefully.

"I want to know what to avoid saying or doing, Emma. And I can't do that without information from you. Can you help me out?"

I suddenly felt very sad. This was a truly lovely man. I didn't want to push him away.

"I'll help you with whatever you like," I said, softly. "I want to get to know you too."

We stared at each other for a moment.

"You mentioned boundaries before," he said, slowly. "What kind of boundaries did you have in mind?"

"Abrasive comments," I replied, immediately. "I want nothing to do with them. They're never helpful. I'm a firm believer in positive feedback, and letting people be."

Luke suddenly had an enlightened look on his face. "What else?"

"Group activities—including families. I'm not particularly fond of my family, and I don't understand why dating someone should automatically thrust said person's family into my life," I said, a little breathless. "I don't need to sit on a bus full of octogenarians to see another country, either. I don't enjoy professional sports, although a college or high school game is fun—once in a while. I don't watch television, but I love movies. And I really have no patience with reunions of any kind. If there are people I'd like to have in my life, they're in my life. Period." I paused. "I like intimacy. Not company."

Would he ask for the check and hustle me out of there?

Luke started laughing. "We're very much alike, Emma."

"Honestly?" I asked, relieved.

The waiter brought us more wine to taste.

"So what do you *like* to do?" Luke asked. The music had started. A svelte woman by the piano began singing a French love song.

"Outdoor sports. Travel. Painting. Reading. Riding my horse. Gardening. Cooking. What about you?"

"Pretty much the same," Luke chuckled. "Except for painting. I find landscaping to be satisfying in that respect."

"Cooking?" I asked, intrigued.

Luke grinned at me. "Come to Williams Sonoma with me some time," he said.

Luke parked in front of my garage and offered to walk me to the door. We went around to the back and stood on the porch, looking at the lake. The moon was waning, but there was plenty of light from the stars.

"This has been a wonderful evening, Luke," I said. "Thank you."

"My pleasure. May I call you again?"

Thank heaven for good manners.

"Yes please." And without thinking, I put my hand up to his face, and drew it down to mine.

CHAPTER FIFTEEN

Qualifying Experts

"So?" Carlie asked. "How was it?"

"You sound like Angela," I complained. "Did you think that I'd knock him into the back of his truck, and have my way with him?"

"Did you?"

"I'm an old fashioned gal, Carlotta. It's going to take a little more than a nice dinner and a few rows on the lake."

"OK, but what do you think so far? What's Luke like? Do you think he's a keeper?"

Why was everyone in such a hurry to get me paired off again so quickly?

I ticked off Luke's positive qualities with my fingers. "He's smart," I said, "reserved and polite. Excellent table manners. Good dry sense of humor. Expresses his feelings without drama. Seems to have some depth of character. Best of all, he's very conscious of behavioral boundaries in relationships."

"Your favorite subject," Carlie replied.

"Look," I retorted, "after what I've been through, I have every reason to be careful."

"You're right, Emma. I'm sorry."

"No problem. By the way, what ever happened with your boyfriend? Kirk?"

Carlie giggled. "Before I had a chance to dump him, he found himself someone new to suck on. Some girl at Brown. He sent me a Dear Carlie text."

"How did you feel about that?"

"Relieved! It's so much easier when someone else does the dirty work."

Annie buzzed me. "The Honorable Terrence Stevenson is holding for you."

"Emma! I can't believe that you and Denise have made this nightmare disappear! It was an extraordinary piece of work, and I'm beyond grateful."

"You are so welcome, Terry, but there were other players besides us."

"Well, I can't thank you enough."

"How did it work out with Phoebe Klein?"

"I wasn't privy to all the details of the arrangement, but I've heard that she will repay the State the twenty dollars with interest, and get a quiet slap on the wrist for her perjury. As to our friend Ms. Pierce…."

"Oh, *please* tell me that she's getting the works!"

"Yes indeed. It will be my pleasure to watch from the sidelines as Attorney Pierce gets her turn in the limelight."

"And yet you don't sound bitter."

"On the contrary. I have news, Emma. I'm leaving the bench, after all. I have been made one of those offers that I would be the proverbial fool to refuse."

"Doing labor litigation?"

"Yes. With Jay Portman's firm in New Haven. Between us, I was less than impressed with the way my so-called colleagues in the

Judicial Department supported me through this ordeal. Or, to be more accurate, threw me under the bus. I feel that I'm more than justified in making this move."

I smiled to myself. I remembered that Terry felt as strongly about loyalty as I did.

"Betrayal is a horrible thing," I said, with feeling. "It sucks the soul out of you. It leaves you no option but to cut any remaining cords and move on."

Terry laughed. "And if there's better money on the horizon," he said, "that's just a bonus."

I took Abby out with me to get the mail. The bundle was unusually large and wedged pretty tightly into the box. I tugged, and a few of the smaller envelopes slipped out and landed on the road. I bent quickly to retrieve them before Abs did. There was a strange postcard—three bare bottomed Sumo wrestlers, mooning the recipient. I turned it over. **BACK OFF BITCH!!** was printed in big square black letters.

Arlene again.

At that moment, my neighbor came by with her spaniel.

"Hello Emma," Jill said. I hastily shoved the postcard into a magazine. Our dogs touched noses, and there was a simultaneous wagging of tails.

"All set for the winter?" Jill asked. "I see you got your wood delivered. Do you have a plow truck lined up? They say that this is going to be a bad one for snow."

"I signed a contract last week," I replied, a little distracted.

"I can't believe we're already in the holiday season," she said, shaking her head. "I feel like I just put the patio furniture out, and now it's time to close up everything again."

"I know what you mean."

"Do you have any special plans for Christmas?" She asked. "I've seen a nice looking man at your door a few times. Is he a beau?"

"Possibly." I said.

"Well, I need to get going on dinner." Jill started to walk back to her house, her spaniel trotting amiably behind her. "By the way, you *have* noticed all the drive-bys that you've been getting, right?"

"What do you mean?"

"Some woman in a black Jeep Cherokee. Dark hair, frizzy. I've seen her about ten times in the past three weeks."

"Any specific time of day?"

"Mornings mostly. After you have left for work. I got her license number."

"Did you? Would you mind texting it to me?"

"As soon as I get home. It's on my fridge."

"Thanks, Jill. I'd really appreciate it."

"Today we're going to start our review before finals in January. Hearsay, credibility, and the qualifying of so-called experts," I told my class. "Recall that in the Connecticut legal world, an expert is defined as someone who possesses knowledge and skill which distinguishes her from ordinary witnesses. The assumption is that she is in a superior position to draw inferences and deliver opinions and conclusions within her field of expertise.

"Qualifying experts is an area which lawyers find particularly bothersome. What exactly is an expert? If someone wears a white coat, or a badge, or hangs up a shingle, or prints impressive business cards, does it guarantee that every statement which comes out of his mouth is a fact?

"Is an 'expert' always right? If an expert renders his professional opinion—should this be considered gospel?"

Hal raised his hand. "Doctors have all that education and training. Doesn't that mean that they know what they're doing?"

I restrained myself. "I have a doctorate. That makes me a doctor. As far as I know, I'm the only teacher at this school who is. Do you assume, therefore, that I am incapable of making a mistake?"

There was chorus of Yeses.

"OK," I said, laughing. "This is a room full of sycophants. Put it another way—ever heard the expression 'Get a second opinion'? Why do you suppose that people do that?"

"Because they want to be sure," Joe said, "especially if it's something big."

"Exactly. But how do you know? Who's right and who's wrong?"

"What if they both agree?" Amy asked. "Doesn't it make what they're saying a fact?"

"Not a fact," Lexie said. "It just means that it's more likely to be the correct answer. Diagnosis is entirely subjective."

A loud "Ass kisser" was bellowed from the back of the room. Therese, Kelly, and Rachel were grinning. I felt a sudden rush of bad temper.

I walked to the back of the room and stood over them. In my heels I was nearly six feet tall. "Let's try another scenario. If my grading is based on forty percent class participation, and a certain three students never opened their mouths, except to jeer and disrupt the discussion, for the entire semester, is it a fact that they are going to fail my class?"

There was a moment of silence, but then Jeanne, a new member of Emma's Spies, ventured to raise her hand. "No, but it's more likely than not that they're going to receive an F on their report cards."

"It certainly is," I agreed.

Joanne and I were working with Joy in the indoor. Joanne had made up a simple impromptu dressage test for me to ride. As she shouted out commands, Joy and I attempted to execute them.

"Start by medium walking a straight line from C to X. Posting trot to V, then pick up a left lead canter. At P, down to a ten meter sit trot circle. Posting trot across the diagonal to S. Sit trot a ten meter circle at S. Posting trot to C. Pick up the right lead canter to F. Sit trot to A. Posting trot a ten meter circle. Medium walk a straight line to X. Halt. Ask her gradually now. Salute."

Joy and I stood squarely at X.

"Good Emma! Joy's got the jumper jitters, so she's really tough with smooth transitions. Remember—don't pull her over—*push* her over. Ride what's underneath you—*not* what's in front of you. Create boundaries with your legs. Your right foot is still slipping a little, but you're getting there! Let's work on some shoulder ins and yielding now."

But we never got any further with the lesson. Frank strolled into the indoor with a young horse—one of his training projects—put him on a lunge line, and took up half the ring while the animal bolted around and around. Joy, clearly affronted by this intrusion, pinned her ears back and reared, lashing out with her front legs.

Joanne suggested quietly that I dismount. She finished the rest of the hour on Joy, working with only about a third of the ring.

That evening there was a message on my home voice mail:

"*Good evening, Attorney Carbury. This is Sergeant DiMarco with the Bridge Hollow Police. We ran that license plate. The vehicle is registered to a Mr. Niles Pierce of Milford. Let us know if we can be of any further assistance to you.*"

That night I went to bed early, with an Agatha Christie and a fire in my room.

I am trotting on Merry down the lane to Zachary's family farm. The trees are bare of their leaves. We pass fieldstone walls that separate pasture and corn fields; now barren and frozen. The road curves round a grove of maples, and there is the house.

The white building appears to be two structures, brought together, like the letter L. Each is two stories, with chimneys rising from the middle, and at each end. A pair of beech trees flank the drive in front of the house. In the distance I can see the barn, and beyond it, several cows and four horses are grazing on hay that has been thrown on the deep snow.

A woman appears at the door. She is tall, and very young. She cradles a child in her arms. A little boy is just behind her, one tiny fist caught in her skirts.

"Are you Hannah?" She asks. "Zachary said that you would come."

Zack had told me to go to his family for news. We could not risk letters coming to the school.

"I am his brother's wife," she explains. "My name is Polly. The baby is Richard. The boy is Benjamin, like his father. The family has been here, on this land, for many years."

But I am impatient for word of Zachary. "Is there a letter for me?" I ask.

"There is." She reaches into the pocket of her skirt. "He tells us that he works hard, and that the food is not good. He has asked me to send warm clothes."

I see Zack's writing and I barely hear her.

My Dearest Hannah….

CHAPTER SIXTEEN

Intelligence

"So I'm finally going to meet the dream man!" Angela crowed. She immediately broke into an off key rendering of the *Hallelujah Chorus.*

"Festive."

"I promise to be on my best behavior, Em. What can I bring for Christmas Day?"

"Why don't you come up Christmas Eve? Unless you have plans?"

"I do actually," she reported. "Leo's taking me to see *The Nutcracker.*"

"Lovely. OK, the menu. How about if you bring a couple of side dishes? Sophie and Julie are doing appetizers. Luke is bringing wine and dessert."

"How are you handling the meat issue?"

"I'm doing fish for Sophie and me, and tenderloin for the rest of you."

There was a pause. "And how are you dealing with the gift issue?"

"We've all agreed to suspend with that particular tradition. No one needs any more stuff."

"Uh huh," Angela sounded skeptical. "And what was Luke's response when you delivered this edict?"

"I think he realizes that it's way too soon in the relationship to be exchanging presents."

"And you haven't...?"

"No," I replied quickly. "And if you keep bugging me about it, I'll hold off indefinitely—just to spite you."

"All right Emma. I just think that you'll be a lot less cranky when you finally...."

At that moment there was a loud crash from the street.

"Ange, I'll have to call you later. Something has happened." Abby was barking furiously.

"Emma!" Carlie yelled from the front hall. "Someone just backed into the gate and took off!"

"Did you see the car?"

"No, just the reverse lights."

"I'll call the Bridge Hollow Police. Maybe one of the patrol cars is in the area."

We went out to survey the damage. "What a mess," Carlie exclaimed. "It will have to be completely rebuilt. Do you think whoever it was actually meant to get another house, and this was a mistake?"

I reached into one of the frozen hydrangea bushes at the top of the driveway. "No, I don't. Look."

The postcard was the familiar picture of three Sumo wrestlers baring their bottoms to the viewer. On the back was written in block letters: **NOW YOU'LL GET YOURS BITCH!**"

"That bloody Arlene!"

Carlie, Lexie, and Julie, with Heather and Jeanne, arrived for one more meeting in my office before the girls left for Christmas break.

Carlie got right down to business. "OK Emma, I've been deep undercover!"

We all laughed.

"Therese is mad at you, by the way—but she isn't holding it against me for some reason. Maybe she likes being captain of a winning team too much. I kiss her big ass on a regular basis—it keeps her happy. Anyway, I think we've got what you need to go to the Board of Directors."

Carlie handed me a manila envelope. Inside were about twenty photos of Therese, Rachel and Kelly, with a group of girls circling around them, as they were clearly scanning new snapshots into the **Get Lexie!** website. "I also have recordings of them talking," Carlie said.

I was stunned.

"This is phenomenal Carlie! Er, you didn't have to engage in anything illegal, did you? I mean, besides recording people without their permission?"

"I didn't pull off a bank robbery, if that's what you mean."

"What about you, Julie?"

"Mom went to the Headmistress, and was totally blown off. Since then, it's gotten worse." Julie's pale face turned pink with distress. "They yell names at me in the halls—follow me to the dorm, laughing behind my back. They humiliate me in class. They're pulling witch stuff out of history books, and making flyers from them. They hand them out when they know I'm going to be in a specific place."

"Don't the teachers do anything to stop this?"

"No. It's like I'm invisible."

Heather produced yet another envelope. "These are from the track team, Ms. Carbury. I have photos, emails, and a few recordings from the locker room in the field house. That's Joan—she does shot put. Heidi and Priscilla are long jumpers. Here they are surrounding Jody in the weight room, slamming her against the wall. These are snaps of Jody in the showers—they posted them on the web."

"Oh my god!" I exclaimed. Full frontal nudity, and very clear. "How old is this girl?"

"She's a freshman," Jeanne replied, "so fourteen, maybe fifteen."

"These young women are looking at child pornography charges," I told them.

"And we can prove who took the photos," Heather said. "That moron Priscilla emailed them to everyone on the team."

"And then she bragged about it at practice," Jeanne added. "They aren't the brightest girls in school."

"Excellent work, ladies. Thank you. Anything new at your end, Lexie?"

"Well, the dance is coming together, and everyone is excited." Lexie began.

"Everyone except the PETs," Carlie added.

"My roommate has asked to be transferred to another dorm, but there are no openings, so she's making my life as miserable as she can. She plays loud music when I'm trying to sleep, steals my food, trashes my closet. I can't possibly study there, so I practically live at the library, if I'm not at Gwen's." She hung her head. "A few of Therese's PETs are on Student Government with me—they're not all jocks. They block everything I try to accomplish. The only good news is that the BHS Social committee is behind me about the dance. On all other issues," she concluded, "my voice—and my vote—are completely useless."

We were all quiet for a moment.

"Carlie's right Lexie," I said, "we have enough to go to the Board of Directors with a formal complaint. The plan is to work on it over the break, so after you are all back, and finals are over—I'm going in."

"When finals are over," Lexie sighed. "That sounds good."

I escorted the girls out to the front lobby. Valerie was conferring with Gerry at the front desk, and they both stopped talking when we appeared. I said my good byes, and turned toward the two women. Valerie waved me over. "This was just delivered for you, Emma," she announced. She indicated a floral arrangement in the Christmas theme—red roses, white amaryllis, carnations, and greens. It was a big vase, with a white bow tied in front.

"Thanks," I said, careful not to open the card in their presence.

"I see that your students have been here again?" Valerie inquired. "Perhaps a last minute review session before vacation?"

"Perhaps," I replied, carrying the flowers in to my office, and closing the door behind me.

Emma,
Looking forward to spending Christmas Day with you and your friends.

All my best, Luke

I sat at my desk and pulled up the Tallmadge Academy for Girls website. I clicked on to 'Alumni Relations' and scrolled down until I found what I was looking for.

Underneath a photo of the Headmistress, Yolanda Gibbs, with Valerie Richardson, was the caption: *TA Alum and local attorney Valerie Richardson finalizes plans for the Founder's Day celebration to take place this spring. Richardson is the 2011-2012 Chair of the Alumni Social Committee.*

"Aha," I said out loud. "Counter intelligence."

After dinner I drove back into town to attend Compline at St. Timothy's on the Green Episcopal Church. Built before the Revolution, the structure was cruciform in shape, with a fieldstone base and a tall white steeple. The stained glass windows had been added after the Civil War. I walked through the old cemetery and up the terrace steps to the front of the church.

At eight thirty the big double doors were opened to the public. All electric lights were extinguished, and hundreds of candles—in sconces, on tables and on the floor—were the only illumination. A large censor was burning incense just in front of the first row of pews. I was the only person inside. I took a seat in the back, to the right of the main aisle.

I had been baptized and later confirmed in the Episcopal Church. I sang in the choir while I was in grade school, and later on in high school, and my first marriage had been an Episcopalian ceremony. Although never a regular at Sunday services, I still occasionally enjoyed Evensong, and Compline. At St. Timothy's the atmosphere was particularly conducive to meditation.

I sat quietly, focusing on the flickering lights. A few more people came in, and took their seats. We could hear the choir practicing in the basement. Just before nine, the choir filed in slowly. They climbed the stairs, and waited in the organ loft behind me, until the bells in the tower chimed nine o'clock.

As the bells finished, the choir began to sing. It was the women's group tonight. As their chanting rose and fell in a cappella cadence, my body seemed to go to sleep. My mind was no longer present in the church.

I am seated at my writing table in the herb room. The windows are dark—almost black—except for the stars. They are reflecting on the river outside. There is no fire, so I wrap my thick wool shawl tightly around my shoulders.

I light a candle, and I prepare to write a letter to Zachary. I want to tell him that he has had his way at last. I am weary of lies and pretense and suffering. I will consent to a new life with him when this terrible war is behind us. I pause to listen. Joshua may be back from town at any moment. We are to gather the boys for an assembly at the church.

My Dearest Zachary....

I pour myself into this letter. Zack can not help but understand me when he reads it.

I melt wax in the candle flame and drip it on to the folded paper. I seal it with my gold ring—the insignia is the triquetra trinity knot—an ancient Celtic symbol. It was passed on to me from my mother, and from her mother before that. The women in my family have been witches for centuries.

Christopher arrives, a little breathless, to take my letter to the post.

It is time to call the boys for church.

Angela arrived at nine o'clock Christmas morning for breakfast. I took her up to the big guest room and showed her the bath down the hall.

"Isn't Carlie going to mind that I'm using her space?" Angela teased, putting her cosmetic bag down on the dressing table.

"She's fine. It's good for her to be back in Vermont with her family after so many months. I got a very nice email from her last night."

"For a teenager, I have to admit—she certainly seems to be aware of other people's feelings. That's rare."

"It certainly is."

Back downstairs we took our eggs and juice to the library and sat by the big windows which faced the lake. Abby trotted in and leapt up on to an ottoman. Angela fed her a piece of bacon.

"I assume that the flowers are from Luke?" Angela asked, noting the big vase. "In lieu of a Christmas present?"

"I think it's more of a hostess gift."

Angela sighed. "When are you going to cut this poor guy some slack Em? As far as I can see, he's doing everything right."

"So far," I agreed. "But we've only been dating a few months. If you discount the rowing—even less."

"What are you waiting for, exactly? Some sign that he's for real—that he really cares about you? Or are you expecting the bomb to drop, so you can say that you were right all along?"

"You're missing the point Angela. I'm not an easy person. You've known me most of my life, right? I'm impatient and irritable, especially if I'm hungry or tired. I don't have a lot of tolerance for stupidity. And I can get mean if I'm crossed."

"So you're worried that Luke will figure this out, and walk?"

"Partly. I don't want to be on a pedestal, carefully behaving in front of him. I'd rather not have to worry about suddenly snapping at him for something, and seeing that look of horror when he realizes that I'm not perfect. I will never be that forbearing, sacrificial lamb that *so* many men want in a woman."

"And you think that Luke has you on a pedestal?"

"Maybe. Nick was really the only man in my life who ever devalued me. Frankly, it was a new experience. Most of the men, including my first husband, tried to turn me into some kind of Super Goddess, and were ultimately devastated to find that I'm just like everybody else. You know what dating is—it's peacocks and peahens, showing their feathers. You never see the bad stuff until it's too late."

We took Abby for a walk. The lake was covered with a frozen layer—not thick enough yet to skate on. The sky was a solid mass of white. Abby stood still and sniffed the air.

"The prediction is for heavy snow tonight," Angela said.

"Yes. But don't worry, I have plenty of food. And wood."

CHAPTER SEVENTEEN

The Headmistress

Yolanda Gibbs invited me to sit in front of the big mahogany desk in her office. I had a sudden flashback to my sophomore year of high school, when I was summoned into the principal's office for telling off a teacher.

"I like to have meetings with each member of the staff in January, Emma," she explained. "I feel that it's a good way to start the new year, prepare for finals, see where we all are." She smiled, without showing any teeth. I reciprocated.

"I have your student evaluations here," she continued. "The response was almost unanimously favorable. Laudatory, in fact. You have made a real hit with your Evidence class."

"That's good to know, thank you," I replied, politely. "I've enjoyed it."

"Almost every one of your students has requested that you stay on, and teach additional subjects. The two most popular suggestions were U.S. History, and English Literature. Can you explain this?"

"I used specific examples in Evidence to make my points regarding hearsay, credibility and the qualifying of experts. We analyzed several important eras in American history, as well as a few of the classic novels. I majored in political science at Vanderbilt, and I minored in English and anthropology. Therefore, I have a solid background in each subject."

"I see. That clarifies the situation. I want you to know that the Board has asked that I make the following proposal to you. We will have an opening in the history department in the fall—Mrs. O'Reilly will be retiring after this semester. The Board would like you to consider taking her place, teaching U.S. History, which is an upper class course. You may continue your Evidence class as well, if you wish."

"I'm very flattered, Ms. Gibbs. How much time do I have to think about this?"

"Oh, until after finals are over, I expect," she said breezily. "There is just one other matter that I would like to discuss with you. As I said, most of your students were enthusiastic about your performance in class."

I knew immediately. Therese was predictable, if nothing else.

"A handful of the young women," she began.

"Three?" I prompted.

"As you say, three of the young women were disparaging in their evaluation. They complained that you showed favoritism in class, and that they felt intimidated, and threatened by you."

How ironic.

"Now, I don't know the particulars. Perhaps you would care to explain?"

"There were nearly twenty juniors and seniors in my class, Ms. Gibbs. Every one of them, with three exceptions, was exemplary in terms of behavior. They came to class prepared. They participated and were respectful—both to myself, and to their fellow classmates. We had many interesting and often lively discussions. However, Ms. Ellis and her two comrades were quite the reverse. They were disruptive and openly abusive to their fellow students— one in particular."

"And who would that be?"

"Alexandra Doyle."

Gibbs smirked. "Ah yes, Ms. Doyle. She's been a busy young lady."

"My understanding is that you have declined to act in this matter."

"There is nothing to act upon, Ms. Carbury." Her voice became hard. "This is a privately funded institution. Ms. Doyle does not have to attend Tallmadge Academy. I have made that fact clear to her, on several occasions." She punctuated her comments with several thrusts of her fountain pen. "Speaking of Vanderbilt—I hear from Ms. Doyle's guidance counselor that you have submitted a recommendation to Vanderbilt to support her application for admittance to that university."

"Correct."

"I also hear that you have had several meetings with Ms. Doyle, as well as other Tallmadge Academy students, in your office in Bridge Hollow."

Valerie. Obviously her loyalty to the Connecticut Bar took a back seat to Tallmadge.

"Also correct."

"What was the purpose of those discussions?"

"Various issues were addressed."

"Including Ms. Doyle's false allegations of bullying?" She sneered.

"You feel no obligation to protect these students, once they are admitted to your school?"

"None whatsoever. A degree from Tallmadge…."

"You mean diploma, do you not? TA is in effect a high school. Your students are minors. You are acting *in loco parentis* as Headmistress of this school."

She waved this detail off. "They don't have to be here," she repeated. "We are one of the oldest academies for girls in this country."

"Yes," I replied, with some impatience. "You said so on Orientation Day. But you do realize that you have a contractual duty to protect these children from foreseeable harm?"

"What contract?" She blustered.

"You really need to be speaking with the school's attorney, Ms. Gibbs. It's not my job to give you free legal advice."

Gibbs leaned forward in her chair, her face frozen in anger. "Answer me this, Ms. Carbury. Did you threaten to fail Ms. Ellis?"

"I did."

"And do you intend to fail her?"

"Let's put it this way. Even if Therese Ellis receives one hundred percent on her final exam paper—however unlikely that would be—she will still fail my class. Forty percent of the grade is participation. This was announced at the beginning of the year—it was also printed in the course description, and on the syllabus. Furthermore, it was approved by the head of the department."

Gibbs was silent, fuming behind her big desk.

I rose from my chair. "Talk to your attorney, Ms. Gibbs. In my opinion, the bullying situation at Tallmadge Academy has risen to crisis level. You need to address the problem immediately, before you are forced to address it. In front of a judge."

"Another threat, Ms. Carbury?"

"By no means, Ms. Gibbs. Just some friendly advice—from a very experienced trial lawyer."

The Book Club met at our office in Westport to discuss Anne Brontë's *The Tenant of Wildfell Hall.* Eliot and Angela shared the expense of Japanese take-out for everyone.

"I remember reading the other two Brontë sisters in school,"

Eliot commented, grabbing a crab and avocado roll. "But Anne is new to me."

Angela checked our schedule. "You're about to become reacquainted with Emily and Charlotte. We've got *Wuthering Heights* next month, and *Jane Eyre* in March."

"What's with the high school required reading, then?" Eliot complained.

"Everyone agreed last spring that we were tired of modern novels and non fiction," Dottie reminded her. "I think you were the one who specifically asked for a little culture."

"Huh. OK, maybe you're right. So who's going to talk about Anne?"

"I will," Denise said. "Dorothy said she'd take Emily next month, and Emma will do Charlotte in March."

"*Jane Eyre* is my all time favorite novel," I explained. "Although *Pride and Prejudice* is a close second."

Angela grinned. "Emma's had a thing for Mr. Rochester since we were kids. All that hot tempered romance, and dark, sulking good looks."

"That's true," I admitted, "but now I'd prefer a man who's just a tad less Byronic."

"Speaking of Byronic characters, I'm going to start," Denise announced, waving a piece of tempura like a baton. "*The Tenant of Wildfell Hall* is Anne's second and last novel. It was published in 1848, under Anne's pen name—Acton Bell. Anne was born in 1820, the last of six children. Her mother, Maria, expired when Anne was less than two years old. The two eldest Brontë sisters, Maria and Elizabeth—aged eleven and ten respectively, died of TB, brought on by the unhealthy conditions at school.

"Anne and her two remaining older sisters, Charlotte and Emily, and their brother Branwell, lived in the isolated Haworth Parsonage on the edge of the Yorkshire moors. Their father, the

Reverend Patrick Brontë, an Irishman, was apparently quite a sturdy fellow—he outlived them all. Anne died of TB in 1849. Of the siblings, she was survived only by Charlotte.

"The sisters' short lives were saddened by numerous early deaths of family members, terrible conditions at school, and the misery of earning their livings as governesses. Anne's first novel, *Agnes Grey*, published in 1847, is loosely based on her own unhappy history as governess to two families. For unmarried, educated women, this was the only respectable career available to them. *Agnes Grey* is esteemed for its examination of the treatment of governesses in the early nineteenth century.

"Left mostly to themselves, the Brontë children lived in a world of their own, derived partly from their geographic isolation, and partly from their voracious reading of gothic fiction and poetry. This material included Shakespeare, Scott, Byron, and *The Arabian Nights*. They entertained themselves by writing and painting, and they even produced a monthly magazine.

"Brother Branwell is important in that his tortured personality is depicted by all three sisters in their novels, and especially by Anne with her character Arthur Huntingdon in *The Tenant of Wildfell Hall*.

"Which brings me to our plot summary.

"The story is related in three parts by Gilbert Markham, in a letter to his sister Rose's husband," Denise continued, "which tells of the events leading Gilbert to meet his wife, Helen. The middle of the book is actually Helen's diary from her first marriage."

"Helen Graham is a young woman with a small son, who arrives as a tenant at Wildfell Hall. Wildfell is a spooky old place—an Elizabethan mansion at the top of a hill—cold and gloomy. It is situated in a lonely, unsheltered spot on the moor. But Helen appears to want the privacy. Close mouthed and mysterious, Helen supports herself by painting landscapes. She is immediately the center of gossip in the small Yorkshire town. Her landlord, Frederick Lawrence, is often seen at her house at night, and Helen's son resembles him.

"Gilbert Markham, a gentleman farmer who lives with his mother and sister, has been courting the vicar's younger daughter, Eliza Millward. But once Gilbert meets Helen, he falls for her, and his interest in Eliza wanes. Eliza and her snooty friend, Jane Wilson—she's after Lawrence—spread scandalous rumors about Helen, whom they perceive as a rival."

"I *love* the description of the Reverend Millward," Dottie broke in, "who is a ponderous ass: 'He was a man of fixed principles, strong prejudices, and regular habits, intolerant of dissent in any shape, acting under a firm conviction that his opinions were always right, and whoever differed from them must be either most deplorably ignorant, or wilfully blind.' One wonders if Anne Brontë was writing of someone closer to home."

"One does, indeed," Denise smiled. "Gossip about Helen mounts, until Gilbert, driven mad with jealousy, attacks Frederick Lawrence with a horse whip. Helen refuses to marry Gilbert, as she is married already, and by way of explanation, hands him her diary.

"Through this document, as part two, we find that Lawrence is Helen's brother, and that he has helped her to run away from an oppressive marriage. Her husband, Arthur Huntingdon, is a Branwell Brontë type—handsome, selfish, dissolute, and violent. We'll see more of him when we read *Wuthering Heights*. Arthur is a wealthy drunk who is jealous of his son and unfaithful to his wife. He is physically abusive to Helen, and openly disparaging of her to his pack of low life friends. But it is only when Arthur begins to corrupt their son that Helen realizes that she has had enough.

"In part three Helen returns to Arthur Huntingdon to nurse him in his final illness. Once free of him, she and Gilbert eventually reconnect and marry."

"I found the last part of the book to be a bit of a let down," Eliot remarked, "given the romance and action of the first two thirds of the novel."

"I agree," I said. "The BBC did a much better job with the movie."

"That was excellent, thanks Denise," Angela said. "All right, what were the major issues in this story?"

"Helen is a real feminist," Eliot announced. "Gilbert's mother babbles on about a wife's duty to please her husband—has poor Rose waiting on her brother—whereas Helen refuses to put up with her husband's behavior and disappears with their son."

"Yes," Dottie agreed. "Helen has spirit. She is a strong minded woman, who is frank about her feelings, to Huntingdon and to Gilbert. For a gentlewoman to work as a professional artist in the early nineteenth century is an amazing declaration of freedom."

"Query whether Helen is permitted to continue her artistic self expression once she is remarried, to Gilbert," Eliot commented.

"I think that's the most important point of the novel," Angela replied. "At that time, under English law, married women had no legal rights. They could not own real estate, or enter into contracts, and they certainly couldn't take their husbands to court for divorce or child custody. Whatever property that a woman had at the time of her marriage immediately came under the control of her husband."

"They were chattel," I said, grimly. "As difficult as it was for me to escape my marriage in the twenty-first century, with no children—imagine what it was like for women two hundred years ago. Had Helen left Arthur openly, she would have been forced to do so without her son, or her money. She wanted to save the little boy from becoming like his father."

"But once Helen remarried?" Eliot asked. "Did the estate that she inherited from her aunt go to Gilbert?"

"I think we are to assume that it did," Denise said.

"So what's to stop Gilbert from behaving in the same controlling, abusive way?"

"That was Helen's conflict," Angela replied.

"My favorite line is Gilbert defending Helen to his sister, who has been repeating Eliza's venomous lies," I commented. "Rose claims that he doesn't know Helen well enough to refute the rumors. He says: 'There is such a thing as looking through a person's eyes in to the heart, and learning more of the height, and breadth, and depth of another's soul in one hour, than it might take you a lifetime to discover, if he or she were not disposed to reveal it, or if you had not the sense to understand it.'" I sighed. "Imagine a man saying something that insightful."

"Especially when the whole community has been poisoned by those two jealous bitches," Dottie added.

"The early Victorians were certainly brutal to women and children," Eliot mused. "We're so spoiled in this century; we forget how far things have come."

"Do you think so?" I asked.

"We have rights on the books," Denise agreed. "We can vote. And own property. We can sue for divorce and be awarded child support. We have advanced degrees and professional licenses. But have the attitudes changed?"

"You mean, do men value women as equals?" Angela inquired.

"Exactly."

"I think that many of them are just giving the laws lip service," Dottie said, bitterly. "My guess is that they are careful what they say, and to whom they say it. It's all an act."

"Teaching teenagers has really opened my eyes," I added. "Just hanging around the boathouse during practice is a learning experience."

"Budding young chauvinists at work?" Angela concluded, handing me a napkin.

"Chauvinists, narcissists, bullies. You name it. And the parents are as bad, if not worse."

"So, how do we stop the cycle?"

"Education," I said firmly. "But obviously that has to start with the schools."

"But, how do we teach the teachers?" Angela asked, rhetorically.

That night I pulled up in my driveway, exhausted from a long day in Westport. I drove into the garage and turned off the motor, listening to the slow cranking noise of the door coming down behind me. I knew that Abby would be anxious for her dinner, but I sat still, breathing. Then I nodded off.

Christopher is waiting for me by Merriment's stall. Despite the cold of the evening, his small white face drips with sweat. I call to the groom, but he does not answer. I lead Merry into her box, and begin to remove her saddle and bridle.

"Mrs. Morrison!" Christopher is panting. "I have just heard something! I must tell you. I cannot believe it is true!"

But I do not hear Christopher's news. Suddenly my husband is there in the door of the barn. It is nearly dark outside, and his tall figure blocks what light is remaining. He must stoop to come inside.

"You—boy! Come here!" Joshua is growling, and in his right hand, I see the whip.

I move quickly to get between them. I attempt to restrain my husband's arm, but he strikes me down. He clamps his hand on Christopher's shoulder. Christopher winces with pain, and they are gone.

I get up slowly. I have banged my hip on the hard floor, and it aches. Merry is lathered and cold, and needs a rub down. I adjust her blanket and throw her some hay.

Joshua is back, but he is alone. He is shivering and wet and wild eyed.

"What has happened to the child?" I demand, terrified.

He regards me with scorn. "I have attended to that little problem," he sneers, "and he is done." He walks over to Merry, who pins her ears back. "Get your horse ready. We are leaving. Tonight."

"Why?" I am in hysterics now, over fear for Christopher. "Tell me."

"The colonies will lose this war, Hannah." His face is blank and dead. He can no longer hide his disdain for our marriage. "The British have destroyed the Continental currency. The French admiral has lost his battle and has turned tail for France. Washington's army is camping in New Jersey—he will never take New York now." He brings his face to within an inch of mine. "And your lover will die."

"What have you done?" I cry, in horror.

"I have been passing information to the British," he replies. "To assure my place on the winning side." He hurries to his horse with a saddle. "Information regarding troop movement, and supply transports through Litchfield." He leads his horse out of the stall. "And tonight I was very nearly caught. But I took care of that little spy. Hurry! We are riding to the coast—there we can get a boat to New York. You have five minutes."

Poor Merry has hardly finished her hay, and we are back on the road. It is dusk. As we gallop south to the main road I glance behind me toward the river, wondering where the body of poor little Christopher lies.

CHAPTER EIGHTEEN

Past Life Karma

I decided that there had to be answers about Hannah and Zack somewhere. The Bridge Hollow Historical Society seemed the most obvious place to start.

The research library was attached to the main museum, with an entrance at the side of the building. According to the plaque on the heavy oak door, this building had once been the home of the town apothecary and his family. I walked up to the counter, mentally crossing my fingers.

The middle aged woman at the research desk was extremely helpful.

"We have several shelves devoted to Judge Morrison and his wife," she said. "No one knows what happened to them—they disappeared in January of 1780. It's a big mystery still, I'm afraid."

I refrained from enlightening her.

"Here's an inventory of the Morrison papers," she continued, handing me a copy. Perhaps you'd like to go through that first. It might narrow your search."

I sat at one of the long tables.

Most of the items had to do with Bridge Hollow School—letters, itemized supply lists, accounting reports, notations regarding staff. I ran my finger down the columns until I found several entries pertaining to Hannah. I froze in my chair.

Hannah Morrison	*Household Accounts Bridge Hollow School (1771 to 1780)*
Hannah Morrison	*Printed Books (various)*
Hannah Morrison	*Commonplace Book (1775 to 1780)*
Hannah Morrison	*Book of Shadows*
Hannah Morrison	*Letter from Zachary MacLaren January 5, 1780*
Hannah Morrison	*Letters from family members (various)*
Hannah Morrison	*Letters from parents of students (various)*

"Here are copies of *The Bridge Hollow News* articles that were printed at the time of the disappearance," the woman said. She laid them on the table. "Hannah never saw many of those letters," she explained. "They arrived after she and her husband were gone. They were kept by the BHS Board of Directors for years, until they finally came to us."

She placed her finger on the third and fourth entries. "These were found by accident, in 1974, when the BHS Library was expanded, and some of the old buildings were refurbished. She had hidden them behind a panel in a closet, in a room off the kitchen. The originals are under glass, but I have copies, if you'd like to see them."

It was an extremely odd sensation, looking at Hannah's handwriting, having been familiar with it for months from my dreams.

I took a deep breath, exhaled, and asked about Zachary MacLaren.

"Oh, he came back from the war, perfectly fine. Not a scratch on him. He was a lawyer in town, and he picked up where he had left off with his practice—eventually did some teaching at BHS. Zachary never married. His brother worked the family farm, and it is still owned by one of his descendents." She paused. "It's pretty obvious from his letter that he and Hannah were lovers. This was found in 1974 with the other things. It was tucked in her witch's book with the last entry—a protection spell for soldiers."

I tried to keep my voice from shaking. "I'd love to buy copies of Hannah's two personal books, as well as the newspaper clippings, and the letter from Zachary."

I sat there, semi conscious, while she printed out what I needed. When she was done, I decided that it was time that I had a long talk with Sophie.

I asked Sophie about past lives.

"You talked about karma in class," I began. "And you mentioned paying off karmic debt from past lifetimes in this life. Would you mind telling me a little more about that? The books aren't particularly helpful."

Sophie looked at me, a thoughtful expression on her face. "Have you been engaged in shamanic journeying lately?"

"No," I replied, a little embarrassed. "Dreams. They started at the same time I began teaching my class on evidence. They stopped just recently."

"What do you remember about them?"

"Pretty much everything," I said, holding up my dream diary. I explained my experiences with Hannah and Joshua Morrison, Zachary, and Christopher.

"And you feel that you were Hannah in these dreams? You're not watching from somewhere else?"

"Oh, I was Hannah," I replied. "No doubt about it. I felt what she felt, and sometimes it was unbearable—the conflict, and the pain that her ambivalence gave her." I shivered. "She truly despised her husband."

"And that's something that resonates with you?"

"Deeply. The creepy thing is that Joshua was *so* much like Nick. Not to look at," I explained. "But they were both former judges. The seemingly pleasant face that is put on for the rest of the world—meaning the male half—as opposed to the dead zone that is the soul. Nick devalued me in public, and he was physically abusive in bed. Joshua beat his wife and brutalized his students. Then he betrayed his country. He was a really nasty piece of work."

"Did the dreams run in a logical sequence, or were they mixed up and choppy?"

"Logical sequence. It was like being an actress in a television series, and I was one of the main characters. Hannah was playing two dangerous roles at the same time."

Sophie was silent for a moment. "I'm not an expert on dream analysis, Emma. But the authorities agree that dreams which have a definite story line are not dreams at all. They are some kind of visit. Especially if the story continues to develop each time."

"Visit? You mean to a past life?"

"Yes. Or possibly, to that of an ancestor."

"I'm confused."

Sophie smiled. "As I said in class, Wiccans believe in reincarnation, meaning that the same soul has returned over and over to this planet, to live out several, or perhaps many lives, in order to experience various emotions, and shed patterns of behavior. Ancestors, however, are spirits of someone in your family—in this life, or in past lives. Their fears and limiting beliefs are like old tapes that keep replaying for their kids and grand kids, until someone turns them off. Families have karma. Even countries have karma. Does that make sense?"

"So Hannah could be anybody?"

"In theory, yes. But again, I'm no expert. What's important is how you feel, and what you were getting from your visits to Hannah's life. We know that she was a real person, right? We learned that on Orientation Day. We also know that she was married to the Headmaster of BHS, that she was a witch, and that they both disappeared toward the end of the war. The important question is—why are you replaying her story? And what triggered it?"

"It all started that first afternoon, after class. I fell asleep in the library—in the big reading room that overlooks the river."

"OK. The triggers could be teaching children, at that school, in that particular part of a specific building. Anything else? Did something happen in class that might be a factor?"

"I was telling the kids about the basic rules regarding hearsay—laying proper foundations of fact, assessing the agenda of the story teller. Never believe anything you hear, and only half of what you see. That kind of thing."

"And what was their reaction to this information?"

"Their young minds were rocked. Most of them admitted to believing everything they're told by the media, and especially if it's posted on somebody's Facebook page. One or two of them were quite belligerent."

"Hmm."

"You're thinking of poor little Christopher?"

"Aren't you? Bullying is alive and thriving at Tallmadge Academy for Girls, as we have seen," Sophie replied, angrily. "Maybe you're the warrior who is meant to make a big change here; start the ripple effect. This may be unfinished business for your spirit to address. A real opportunity to heal. Perhaps Hannah, hampered by being a woman, and a witch in the late 1770s, couldn't achieve what you can now. The risk was too great. You're a trial lawyer—one who sued her abusive former judge husband and prevailed." Sophie's face relaxed. "As an added bonus, you're learning witchcraft. There are all kinds of triggers going on here. Time to repay some karmic debts."

"Do you think that Joshua was Nick in a former life?"

"It's possible, Emma. Or one of his ancestors. One theory is that spirits tend to evolve in groups—meaning that they return to the earth together, life after life, playing out different roles. Rather like travelling theater troupes who write their own scripts."

I asked the question that was foremost in my mind. "And Zachary? Where does he fit in to my big learning curve?"

"You're the one who cast the love spell. You tell me! My guess is that Hannah's decision was the wrong one, so her soul had to repeat the lesson. Here you are!"

This was a bit too much pressure, even for me.

"What is the meaning of the triquetra on Hannah's ring?"

"In Latin triquetra means 'three cornered,' and tends to be used as a symbol of anything that is threefold. Christians have used it to represent the Holy Trinity—some claim that it recalls the shamrock of St. Patrick. Wiccans use it as a symbol of protection, or to represent the three phases of the goddess, or moon—maiden, mother, and crone. The number three was considered to be very powerful in ancient times. The circle—sometimes seen running through the three interconnected loops of the triquetra—represents the unity of the three elements—land, sea, and sky."

"The Halliwell sisters had it on the cover of their Book of Shadows, as I recall." In my opinion, Paige had the most valuable powers. She could move objects with her mind—telekinesis—and she could 'orb'—or transport herself, and anyone else—to any location. She was also a healer.

"Ah yes. The *Charmed* Ones. There the triquetra symbolized the power of three, acting as one. Their strongest spells required the unified energy of all three sisters."

"*The power of three will set us free*," I murmured.

"Lastly, the triquetra is also considered to be a symbol for lovers, and the threefold promise of relationship—love, honor, and protect. It's common to see a triquetra engraved on a wedding ring, especially in countries where the Celtic tradition is still strong."

"As in Scotland, Wales, and Ireland."

"And Cornwall. Also Brittany in France."

There was a pause. I felt that Sophie was gathering energy to say something to me.

"Carlie's right, Emma. It's time that you opened up to someone. Don't make Hannah's mistake. Don't miss out on the love of your life. That's what really matters—it's why we're all here. The rest of the stuff that people worry about is just nonsense. Cut your energetic cords with the past. What are you afraid of?"

I fought the urge to shout at her. "Isn't that obvious? Another Nick. Another phony charmer with no substance, but plenty of agenda. I'm holding out for that one true person who accepts me as I am—not as what he needs."

"From what I observed on Christmas Day, you have the perfect man just waiting for a sign from you," Sophie replied. "You've already asked the Universe for what you want in a life partner. It's been sending you signals for months. Just relax, shut off your hyper vigilant brain, and jump in."

I laughed. "Let Luke know, you mean? All right."

5th January 1780

My Dearest Hannah,

By the time your letter reached me, I had begun to fear that I would never hear from you. I speak to you every day—in my mind and in my heart.

The days here are wearisome. We are short of food,
of clothing, of blankets. We are half starved—often
times eating what food there is for the horses. The
roads and rivers are clogged with snow and ice. The
nerves of the men are strained. The army is greatly
reduced in number—the expiration of so many
short enlistments—many fear that the army is on
the point of dissolution.

But as I write to you, I am in the toils of some
feverish dream. You insist that we keep a distance
between us, but often times I feel you—a heart beat
away. Chance has offered us a measure of happiness
Hannah. My attachment to you grows stronger
each day. I am assured that we may live and love
across the miles between us, until I am home once
more. I only wish I could hold you in my arms.

Forgive this hasty scrawl, tho' my words are warm
from the heart of your loving

Zachary MacLaren

I pulled my BlackBerry out of my purse, and asked Luke if we could meet for dinner that evening.

Luke read through the copied pages of my dream diary while I played with my appetizer and finished my martini. When he looked up, I handed him the Historical Society's inventory of Hannah's papers. Finally, I handed him a copy of Zack's letter.

"You've been having these dreams since September?" He asked, clearly amazed.

"Yes. On and off. You should know that this isn't a new experience for me," I began. "That is to say, I'm used to my dreams being jam packed with information. I've never dealt with past lives before, though."

"And you think that Hannah is you in a past life?"

"Or one of my ancestors, yes."

"I already knew about Zachary," he said thoughtfully. "He's definitely an ancestor. Is it possible that he is also a past life for me as well?"

I took a deep breath. "Possibly. Sophie wasn't sure. There's no real handbook for this kind of thing. But it seems to fit."

"Because of you and me?"

"And Joshua, who is frighteningly like my ex husband."

Luke was shocked. "Not a traitor who strikes his wife and murders small children!"

I shook my head. "Just his demeanor—his disdain. His arrogance regarding his position, and his complete disregard for his wife as a life partner. And the sad thing is Luke, I don't see that things have changed much in two hundred and thirty years."

"Is that why you always keep me at a distance?" Luke asked.

I was stunned, and immediately became defensive. "Do you mean because I haven't dragged you off into a back bedroom somewhere, like Hannah did to Zack? Are you talking about sex?"

"No!" Luke nearly shouted. Several tables in our vicinity stopped their conversations and stared at us.

"Sorry," he said, lowering his voice. "I'm talking about the way Zack feels about Hannah. Read it again, Emma. Please. That's what I've been trying to say to you—what I feel. How I would like this to go. If you would only allow it."

I felt numb with fear. And then I burst into tears.

"We're never going to be allowed in that restaurant again," I worried, after we had returned to my house, and were sitting in front of a good fire.

"Sure we will. They've been clients for years."

I moved close to him and he put his arm around me. Abby, feeling left out, jumped up and took her usual position on Luke's lap.

"Where do we go from here?" He asked.

"I want to fix Hannah's mistake," I said. "I promise you—if you can handle a slow and easy does it kind of pace—that I will make it worth your wait. On all fronts," I added, grinning.

"Fair enough," he said.

Abby suddenly picked up her head, sniffed, and took off for the front hall, barking frantically. We followed her.

A fire was burning in the middle of the lawn. I could see a dark shape moving quickly toward the road.

Luke ran outside with Abby, while I called the police.

I had just gotten the Bridge Hollow dispatcher on the line when I heard a squeal of tires and a loud thud. I reported the information at high speed and hurried out the door.

Arlene Pierce had backed her car straight into my neighbor Jill's pickup truck. Jill and Luke were talking to a police officer, while her partner was putting Arlene in the back of the patrol car.

"Are you all right?" I asked Jill.

"Yes, thanks. This truck is a tank. Good thing I had my seat belt on."

"What happened? It looks like she was trying to turn into your driveway."

"She was. But she didn't see me coming from the other direction. The police were here almost immediately. It was amazing."

"I asked them to keep an eye out for a few days. I was worried that Arlene would try something a little extra this time."

"Good decision."

"You know this woman Emma?" Luke asked in surprise. He was holding Abby, who was growling ferociously.

"Oh yes. Arlene has been a bit of a problem lately. But the situation appears to be under control now." I took his arm. "Worried Luke?"

"Of course not. Life's more fun with the occasional shake up. Keeps things interesting."

I had lunch with Denise on Friday.

"I hear that our buddy Arlene is finally going to get what she deserves."

"It was a long time coming, wasn't it?"

"I saw Phoebe in court the other day. She's ecstatic. She said to say hello to you."

"I'm glad if she's happy. She seemed like a kind soul."

Denise scowled. "It's the kind souls who are easy targets for psycho bullies like Arlene."

I grinned. "Only if the bully gets away with her behavior, and this one sure didn't." I replied, jubilant.

"Yeah, victory is a good thing."

"It's sad though, Denise. Remember what Randy told us about kids who were bullied? How they often grow up to be bullies themselves? Incest is probably the worst form of bullying out there. Arlene was a victim."

"True. But Arlene is now an adult and a trial lawyer. She's worked with these cases for years. She's had every opportunity to help herself," Denise argued. "Compare her to you. Similar childhoods, but you did your emotional work. Don't feel too sorry for Arlene, Em."

After lunch I checked my messages.

Carlie's voice was frantic.

"Emma, where are you? You need to get here fast. Lexie just got expelled."

CHAPTER NINETEEN

Expelled

Carlie had moved Lexie into my small guest room. Lexie was lying on the bed near the window wrapped in a blanket. The hood from her track team sweat shirt was pulled over her head. Abby was stretched out across her lower legs, nose between her paws.

Carlie pulled me into her room. "She's pretty bad Emma," she said, quietly. "I told her that I'd stay here too. Sophie's bringing Julie over after her last exam. I hope that's OK."

"It's perfect, honey. You've done great. Uh, do you think that Lexie will talk to me now, or do you know the story?"

"Let's try her together," Carlie replied. "I can fill in the gaps."

"My art history final was this morning," Lexie explained. I had brought her a cup of chamomile tea, and Carlie had convinced her to sit up. Abby was now lying beside Lexie, her head on Lexie's lap. "It was my last exam, and I was looking forward to relaxing a little this weekend, before classes start again on Wednesday. I love art history, and I was totally prepared for this test. Mrs. Grafton gave us the visual portion first—we had to look at a slide show of paintings, and give the title, artist, and date. Then she turned off the computer, and left the room. That's when it started."

Lexie's eyes welled up, and her face turned red. She rolled on her side and began to sob.

Carlie placed a hand gently on Lexie's shoulder, and continued the story. "There were six PETs in this class, Emma, including Therese."

I couldn't help myself. "Therese was learning about art?"

"That's what I said. Anyway, the teacher leaves the room, and Kelly and Therese start in on Lexie. They shout at her that she is a retard and a slut, and that she is too much of a low life to go to TA. They say that they consider it their mission for the rest of the year to get her thrown out of school. Lexie said that she tried to block their voices, and concentrate on the essay part of the test, but it was just too awful for her. Eventually Mrs. Grafton comes in to collect every one else's papers. She tells Lexie to go into the next room to finish up—Lexie gets an extra fifteen minutes for exams.

"Lexie said that by then she was in a kind of fog. She said that she doesn't remember picking up her test booklet, or walking through the door, or sitting down in a chair."

"Traumatized," I murmured.

"The next thing she's aware of—she's in the Headmistress's office, turning herself in for cheating."

I gasped.

"What happened after that?"

Lexie appeared to regroup.

"Ms. Gibbs called my advisor, Mrs. Furling, and the Deputy Headmistress, Ms. Collier. They all sat around the Headmistress's room, talking about me, while I waited in the secretary's office. Then they brought me back in, and told me that I was expelled from Tallmadge Academy. I was to leave the school today, with my things."

"But your family lives in St. Louis! Where did they imagine you would go?"

"They said that they'd book me a room at the Bostwick Tavern. They said that they'd call my parents. They also said—they said that...."

"They said that they would be immediately notifying Vanderbilt of her expulsion," Carlie finished for her, "so that Lexie would no longer be considered for admission."

"Gibbs got off on it too—the bitch!" Lexie exclaimed. "It was so obvious that screwing my chances with Vandy was her favorite part of the whole thing."

Another Queen Bee bully.

"So Lexie went to my room first—luckily I had just finished my French final. We ran down to Julie's—she called her mom—I called you—and here we all are," Carlie concluded. They both looked at me. "So now what?" Carlie demanded.

"I need to talk to your parents, Lexie."

She gave me her mother's cell number. "They're flying out here on Sunday," Lexie said.

"Good, but we need to get on the ball—now. Please make yourself comfortable. Carlie knows where everything is. Order takeout if you're hungry. I have a few calls to make."

On my recommendation, Tina Rosen was hired by the Doyle family to meet with the attorney for Tallmadge Academy. They had their conference in Jeff Merton's office in Danbury. With her clients' permission, Tina gave me a briefing via the telephone that afternoon.

"The man's a moron Em!" Tina raged. "You were right! These people see TA as some kind of hallowed institution—the young women, as he calls them, are lucky to be getting an education there, and they are certainly free to leave at any time. Apparently the administration has a long waiting list of rich girls, just dying to be enrolled. Merton kept talking about a 'degree from Tallmadge,' until I pointed out that TA is just a jumped up high school with big bills, and an even bigger attitude. I had to keep reminding the turkey that these girls were minors."

"That's pretty bad, coming from a lawyer."

"You haven't heard the worst part!" Tina snorted with disgust. "When I informed him that the school had a contractual duty to stand in as parents for these children—*in loco parentis*—his response was: What contract?"

"You're kidding! Did this guy go to law school?"

"Maybe he was out sick with a hangover the day they learned about implied contracts."

"Not to mention duty, breach, causation, and damages in Torts."

"Yeah. He was pretty fuzzy on that stuff too. When I brought up the fact that Lexie has been diagnosed with ADD, and as a disabled American is entitled to file her civil rights case in federal court—he sputtered for a while, and then got downright nasty."

"So what's our next step? Do you want to take a shot at talking to the Board of Directors?"

"Definitely. First, we want to keep this situation out of the press, if possible. Second, we'd like to get Lexie reinstated before anyone has noticed that she's gone."

"And third, the Board needs to be hit over the head with the fact that Lexie is just one of many, and they are damned lucky if someone doesn't get hurt."

"My thoughts exactly. You know what this means Emma?"

"Yes I do. It's time for Emma's Spies to step up to the plate."

We assembled in my library, with Tina running the meeting. Abby prowled around the room, sniffing at various plates, while Sophie and I refilled them with pizza and salad.

It was a large group. Heather and Jeanne had brought five girls from the track team, including Jody, whose nude shower photo had upset us so much at the last meeting. Lexie's dorm monitor, Gwen—the college student who had hit a wall with the TA administration—had eagerly consented to attend. "My job's a joke," she said.

Two of the Student Government officers joined us. Lexie beamed at them to show her appreciation.

The surprise came when Luke arrived with two of the men that I'd met from the Masters team. Henry Judson had with him his daughter Carole—a freshman at Tallmadge. And Phil Deming, a BHS alum, announced to Tina that he had some information that might be helpful to our cause.

Lexie's parents, Mr. and Mrs. Doyle, sat with Lexie on the big couch by the fireplace.

Tina finished her slice and called the meeting to order.

"My first question is extremely important. How many of the students here are legal adults?"

One of the SGA officers, two track athletes, and Jeanne raised their hands.

"OK, thanks," Tina said, taking down their names. "Most of you are minors then. Lexie, Carole, and Julie have parental units here with them. Do the rest have written permission from their parents to be here, and if necessary, testify?"

Emails fluttered as Tina collected them.

"Excellent. Let's begin. Those of you who are members of Emma's Spies have produced an unbelievably comprehensive record in favor of our position. As an attorney, I can honestly say that I have rarely seen such a thorough job of discovery, even by professionals. Well done."

"We had a great teacher!" Heather said.

There was loud clapping, especially from the Doyle family. Luke, sitting next to me, nudged my shoulder and grinned.

"The closed hearing with the Tallmadge Academy Board of

Directors will take place on Tuesday night, in the auditorium. This will be an informal opportunity for us to present evidence and make arguments. The good news is that we will be able to use the information that the Spies have gathered. I'm only going to give them a juicy sample," Tina added. "One never shoots all of the arrows from one's quiver."

"We could always threaten to post it all on the web," Carlie suggested.

There was laughter.

"Gentlemen," Tina said, turning first to Henry. "I'm very interested in what you have to tell us."

"I can report to you what I have observed of the girls' team when I've been at the boathouse in the afternoons. More importantly, my daughter Carole, who is a freshman at TA and a new member of the Tallmadge rowing team, has a story to relay."

Carole was a sturdy looking redhead with a cheerful face and bright green eyes. Carlie had told me that she was one of the promising newcomers, and a powerful oar.

"Therese likes to show everyone who's boss," she said, "and she's especially tough on the new kids. I've seen her throw girls off the dock, whack them with oars, trip them while they're carrying boats." She paused, clearly embarrassed in front of the men. "She's horrible in the locker room. She and her gang make fun of people's bodies—how they look in Lycra—comments about, um, you know."

"Bra sizes?" Sophie suggested.

"Uh, yeah. Thanks. That's the worst part, because you can't get away from her easily in the locker room—especially if you're in the shower."

"I have audio and visual of her doing this stuff," Carlie said, helpfully. "Carole's right. It's bad."

"Have you ever been the target, Carole?" I asked.

"No. But I've tried to stand up for other kids who have, and I got 'the talk' from Rachel and Kelly."

"Meaning?" Tina asked.

"Oh you know. They said that I was good for the team, but they could replace me if they had to. They tried to explain that they were just weeding out the bad rowers to benefit the rest of the group."

"Basically BS," Carlie added. "I've had the same lecture. It's all about keeping you in your place. Scared and silent."

"Thank you ladies." Tina turned to Phil Deming. "Next?"

"Luke and I were rowing at BHS when Yolanda Gibbs was a student at Tallmadge. She was two years ahead of us, and she was captain of the rowing team."

I felt the tingle of something big coming in.

Luke turned to me. "Were you aware that in our day, Yolanda was the leader of the PETs?"

Tina dropped into a chair. Her courtroom demeanor was lost in the shock. "Are you KIDDING me?"

"Nope," Phil said. "And compared to Yola, this Therese sounds like a cream puff."

Tina was speechless. I picked up the thread.

"Is there any way that we can prove this?" I asked.

"Oh sure." Gwen stood up and walked to the windows to stand by Tina. She was carrying a black binder. "I have her picture right here."

Tina and I gaped at each other. Gwen flipped some pages, and handed the book to Tina.

The binder was a manual for dormitory monitors. There was a list of chapter headings in front, including the more prosaic concerns such as laundry rooms and bathrooms, roommate conflicts, and the evils of hot plates and microwaves. Then—the touchier issues, such as lesbian activity, boys in the dorm, and hints of aberrant behavior among the residents.

The last chapter was entitled The Protectors and Enforcers of Tradition. The chapter began by outlining the history of the PETs—the group began in the 1870s as a social sorority called the Rosebuds, and by the time of World War II, had evolved into a secret society with one aim: keep the students loyal to Tallmadge Academy, and faithful to its traditions.

In 1952 there had been a tragedy at TA. A junior named Anna Crawford, who had been complaining of headaches and stomach problems for most of the year, drowned herself by jumping off the Woodruff foot bridge in the middle of the night. Her body had been found the next afternoon, by the BHS rowing team.

The school had circled the wagons—its staff muzzled, and its students threatened with expulsion if they talked. Anna's parents had taken her away quietly, and the sterling reputation of Tallmadge Academy had remained untarnished. The PETs had begun their reign of terror.

The photos started with the 1955 gang—about ten female Fonzies, in leather jackets and biker boots. The shots from the sixties were humorous—beehive hairdos, tight black turtlenecks, and leather mini skirts.

Gwen had tabbed the group shot for the 1982-1983 academic year.

And there was Yola Gibbs in the center of the photograph.

"Is that a riding crop in her hand?" Carlie asked, disgusted.

"Complete with tall boots and breeches," I replied. "She's an equestrienne. I should have known."

"She carried that whip everywhere," Phil remembered. "The guys used to get a big laugh out of it."

"Never saw her with a guy, though," Luke added.

"That answers a question that I had!" Julie said suddenly, and everyone laughed, even Lexie.

Tina finally recovered her poise. "I think we're good to go here, people. If you give me half an hour, I'll decide on the witness list for next week." She paused. "And if I ever consider opening an investigation agency, you're all hired."

Sophie had stayed to help me clear up.

"I've been thinking about poor Anna Crawford," I said, piling up plates and retrieving napkins.

"And little Christopher from your dreams?"

"Of course. Do you think there's a connection?"

"It seems fairly obvious to me, Emma. All that terrible energy—swirling around these two schools like a black fog. Frankly, it's amazing that there haven't been more tragedies."

I went to my desk and pulled out the information I'd received from the Historical Society. "Here's the news article regarding the finding of Christopher's body," I said, handing her the file. "It's very sad. No one came forward to claim him—his brother William was on Manhattan with the British. So the town buried the boy."

Sophie read the clipping.

"What I find odd," she said, "is that the reporter didn't make a connection between Christopher Marsh's death, and the mysterious disappearance of the BHS Headmaster and his wife."

"Hushed up," I replied. "It wouldn't look good for the school."

"But there must have been talk, Emma. My guess is that the locals assumed the matter had more to do with Hannah—her love affair with Zachary, her practicing witchcraft, or both."

"So Joshua looked like the brave husband? Protecting his wife by spiriting her off—where? If they'd been patriots, wouldn't someone have heard from them? Wouldn't it make more sense to assume that they were Tories? That they escaped to New York and eventually got on a ship to London?"

Sophie nodded. "That does seem logical. But these people were at war on their own land—something this country hasn't experienced since the 1860's. They were in survival mode, and I'd bet that a lot of details just slipped through the cracks."

I sighed. "Just like Anna Crawford. Do you think that she was a victim of bullying as well?"

"It certainly sounds like it. But, we'll never know. Whatever was going on with Anna before she made her terrible decision, if in fact her death *was* a suicide—two things are clear. First, the Tallmadge administration was aware of the problem, and second, the school wasn't concerned about dealing with Anna—until it was too late."

Joy and I attempted to spend some time together in the indoor arena. It was a cold, windy day, and the noise from the snow blowing off the metal roof was scaring the horses. There were too many riders in the ring, as usual. The farm maximum was six at a time, but when even one horse was jumping a course, it created chaos for everyone else.

Millie was on her big Swedish warmblood—Rebel. New to riding at the age of sixty, Millie was taking lessons and occasionally trucking Rebel off the premises for hunter paces, and even the occasional hunt. She had a tendency to ride in her own world— forgetting arena rules such as pass on the left, yield to riders taking lessons, and no walking on the rail.

Frank was leaning against the gate end of the ring, bellowing directions at his two jumper students, and monopolizing the entire space. Three of us, including my trainer, Joanne, were huddled in one corner, attempting to stay out of the way. "I don't know what to do," Joanne murmured to me.

Millie, oblivious as ever, was hand galloping around the periphery, right in the path of Frank's students. One of them, approaching a jump, had to pull up to avoid running into Rebel.

Frank went ballistic. Shouting profanities, he charged over to Millie, waving a lunge whip. Rebel—terrified—reared, which dumped Millie on to the footing with a painful thud. Rebel then took off on his own around the ring. Joy snorted and skittered sideways, her ears flat on her neck. I sat up straight and spoke to her quietly. Rory, the assistant barn manager, came running into the ring, and grabbed Rebel's bridle. Millie still lay there on the ground in a fetal position, the wind knocked out of her. Frank hovered over her person, waving the whip. I considered dismounting when Meredith, the owner of the farm, coolly walked in and sashayed over to Millie.

Meredith stood next to Frank, her mouth clenched. "You've been warned about barn rules, Millie," she said. "This is the last time. You have forty-eight hours to get your belongings, and your horse, off of my property."

"Unbelievable!" I said to Joanne, as Millie hobbled out of the ring, head bowed. Rory followed with Rebel.

"Yes, Emma," Joanne said quietly. "Meredith knows that hers is the only game in town—the one farm with an indoor, anyway. The other options are twenty or more miles away."

"That's all very well, Joanne," I replied. "But if the only way to use the indoor safely is to get here at six in the morning, I hardly see the point."

That night I went online and researched the definition of a Commonplace book.

A Commonplace book was a blank book in which one copied out memorable prose, quotations, or poetry—including sermons and hymns—which reso-nated with the reader, or attracted his or her admi-ration. Such a practice would fix these words in the mind of the reader. It was also used as a method of improving penmanship.

I had started my own Commonplace book nearly two decades previously, not knowing that my habit of recording favorite quotations had been practiced for centuries. I was a law student at the time—and feeling the need for more positive energy, and inspiration, in my life. I opened my little book to the first page.
The first entry was dated January 2, 1991.

There are three marks of a superior man:
being virtuous, he is free from anxiety;
being wise, he is free from complexity;
being brave, he is free from fear
Confucius

After that, my entries, always quotations, were regular, with two distinct themes. I flipped quickly through the pages.

Give us grace and strength to forbear and to
persevere—give us courage—and the quiet mind.
Robert Louis Stevenson

True friendship can afford true knowledge.
It does not depend on darkness and
ignorance.
Henry David Thoreau

We never know how high we are
Til we are called to rise.
Emily Dickinson

One of the deep secrets of life is that all that is
really worth doing is what we do for others.
Lewis Carroll

Knowledge is the antidote to fear.
Ralph Waldo Emerson

When words lose their meaning,
people lose their freedom.
Confucius

One word frees us of all the weight and
pain of life: That word is love.
Sophocles

Love conquers all things; let us too surrender to Love.
Virgil

For love casts out fear, and gratitude
can conquer pride.
Louisa May Alcott

I consider everybody as having a right
to marry once in their lives for love.
Jane Austen

Courage is the price life extracts for granting peace.
Amelia Earhart

And the final entry, just before my Juris Doctorate was conferred in May of 1993:

No Coward Soul is mine
No trembler in the world's storm-troubled sphere
Emily Brontë

Courage and love. Nearly twenty years before, those were the two emotions foremost on my mind. Was courage an emotion? Perhaps one could not have one, without the other.

I picked up my copy of Hannah's Commonplace book and glanced through the first few pages, suddenly curious. What words had inspired her? The country was at war with Britain, she was stuck in an abusive marriage, and she was passionately in love with a man who had wanted to run away with her, and start a new life in Boston.

16 June 1775

If we wish to be free—if we mean to preserve inviolate those inestimable privileges for which we have been so long contending—if we mean not basely to abandon the noble struggle in which we have been so long engaged, and which we have pledged ourselves never to abandon until the glorious object of our contest shall be obtained—we must fight!

Patrick Henry
Give Me Liberty or Give Me Death
23 March 1775

30 March 1776

Perhaps the sentiments contained in the following pages, are not yet sufficiently fashionable to procure them general favor; a long habit of not thinking a thing wrong, gives it a superficial appearance of being right, and raises at first a formidable outcry in defense of custom. But the tumult soon subsides. Time makes more converts than reason.

As a long and violent abuse of power, is generally the Means of calling the right of it in question (and in Matters too which might never have been thought of, had not the Sufferers been aggravated into the inquiry) and as the King of England hath undertaken in his own Right, *to support the Parliament in what he calls* Theirs, *and as the good people of this country are grievously oppressed by the combination, they have an undoubted privilege to inquire into the pretensions of both, and equally to reject the usurpation of either.*

. . . .

The cause of America is in a great measure the cause of all mankind. Many circumstances hath, and will arise, which are not local, but universal, and through which the principles of all Lovers of Mankind are affected, and in the Event of which, their Affections are interested.

. . . .

Thomas Paine
Common Sense / Addressed to the Inhabitants of America
14 February 1776

23 August 1776

. . . .

But when a long train of abuses and usurpations, pursuing invariably the same Object evinces a design to reduce them under absolute Despotism, it is their right, it is their duty, to throw off such Government, and to provide new Guards for their future security.

. . . .

The Unanimous DECLARATION of the thirteen
united STATES OF AMERICA
4 July 1776

Whatever else Hannah Morrison was at the time of her disappearance, she was certainly a Patriot.

CHAPTER TWENTY

Luke's Farm

Luke had invited Abby and me to a winter picnic on his farm. It was as though I had returned to Hannah's ride on Merry, only this time I was awake, and driving my Audi, with my terrier in my lap. The sign on the gate said 'Loarn Farm,' in black Celtic looking script. A sprig of mountain laurel had been painted underneath the name. I made a mental note to ask Luke about the meaning. We passed fieldstone walls that separated the pastures from the corn fields—now cut down to yellowish brown stubble. The drive curved around a grove of maples, and the house appeared, just as it had in my dream.

The white building might have been originally two structures, brought together, like the letter L. Each section of the house was two stories, with the high pointed roofs so common with New England salt box style houses. I counted four chimneys. The ancient beech trees were still flanking the drive—they were now immense. Behind the house I could just make out the barn, and beyond it, various animals were grazing on hay. I saw three horses—one chestnut, the other two gray, in one corner of a large paddock.

At the edge of the property, the Litchfield hills rose suddenly—grayish purple and beautiful in the winter light.

Luke came out of the house as we drove up, followed by a white bull terrier.

"This is Rufus," he said, introducing us. I let Abby out of the car. The two terriers sniffed each other, registered approval, and took off toward the barn together. "She'll be fine," Luke laughed. "Rufus is a gentleman."

I grinned. "May I meet your horses?" I asked, priorities well set.

"This way."

We crunched along the path. Looking down, I noted that we were both wearing the same L.L. Bean boots—fleece lined. Mine were navy, his were brown.

"Before I forget Luke, what's the meaning of the name of your farm?"

"Family lore, going back to the year 503, when a young man named Loarn, or sometimes Laurin, came over from Ireland and founded Argyll, in Scotland, with his two brothers. The theory is that the name originated with St. Lawrence, a priest, who was martyred in 258."

"Aha."

"Eventually Clan MacLaren took possession of land in Perth—in the Midlands region—where it remained prominent. However, the family name is also associated from very early on with Tiree, which is one of the islands in the Inner Hebrides."

"Oh! I've been out there—to Mull, Iona, and Skye—but not to Tiree. Have you?"

"No," he replied. "But I intend to. Some day."

"And the mountain laurel?"

"A Clan symbol. Wild laurel is said to provide protection and strength."

We passed the barn, and moved toward the paddock, which had been partially cleared of snow. To my right there was another paddock, which included a large pond. The horses trotted to the gate to greet us. Behind them six goats of varying breeds continued to munch their hay. I began visualizing Joy out there with them. How would she react to goats?

"The chestnut is Hamish," Luke explained. "He's some kind of warmblood, about seventeen hands. I got him from a family who was moving back to the city, and wanted a good home for him. He's still pretty young, maybe seven or eight, but a very good boy under saddle. I haven't tried jumping him yet.

"These two," he continued, patting each big gray in turn, "are Penelope and Nemo. They are part draft, about twelve and thirteen years old respectively, and were originally trained to drive as a pair. They're just ridden now. They're both sensible and comfortable— excellent on trails. Penelope will jump, quite high, actually. Nemo seems to prefer to go around obstacles, if he can."

"Hmm," I mused. "Have you tried setting up some jumps in the paddock?"

"No," he said. "Would you like to help me try that at some point?"

"Of course!" I replied, patting Nemo. "If he really doesn't like jumping, he'll avoid them. But if it's the rider he's worried about— maybe a bad past experience—he'll want to show off on his own."

Abby and Rufus appeared from the other side of the barn. They raced under the fence, and ran out to cavort with the goats. I held my breath, but Abby followed Rufus' admirable example, and showed respect for their much bigger playmates.

"Hungry?" Luke asked. "Lunch is over here."

A circular bench surrounded a huge old oak. Luke had shoveled a path through the snow, and had set up a folding table and tablecloth. A fire was burning in a portable pit with domed screen. There were big sandwiches, hot soup, pasta salad, and chocolate chip brownies for dessert. "This Thermos has mulled cider in it, if you're interested."

I held out a mug.

I noted a cottage, white clapboard like the rest of the buildings, set back on the other side of the paddocks. Smoke was rising from the chimney in the center. "Is that where your staff lives?"

Luke nodded. "Ryan and Patty Hubbard. They're young—early thirties. Absolutely indispensible. Patty made the brownies." He added. "She takes care of the house—the laundry, food shopping—everything. Ryan works the farm. They both help with the animals. I couldn't function without them."

"What do you do with the corn?"

"I sell it locally for cattle feed. We also do our own haying. My long range plan is to put in a real commercial greenhouse, and grow organic vegetables. There's plenty of compost. I'm also thinking about chickens."

"What do the goats produce?"

Luke grinned. "Just fun. They're good company for the horses."

I looked at the long lines of fieldstone walls that disappeared into the tree line. And further back, the incredible purple blue-gray of the hills.

Without thinking, I let out a big sigh of contentment.

"Like it?" Luke asked.

"It's heaven," I admitted, "in a way that's totally different from my place on the lake. You can't see another house, or hear another soul. Not even the cars on the road. You're surrounded by trees and hills and happy animals. How many acres do you have?"

"About two hundred—but some of that is forested."

I digested this.

"Want to see the barn? Patty will be out in a bit to clear lunch."

The dogs followed us as we walked back down the path, and through the big double doors. Inside was cheerful and open, with sun coming in from the cupola, and skylights. The main aisle had sixteen stalls—eight on each side—twelve by twelve feet in size.

"I rebuilt most of this," Luke explained. "It was falling down, and frankly unsafe. I widened the windows and took out some of the original stalls to make the remaining ones bigger. Here's the wash stall, and the feed room next door. The tack room and bathroom are at the other end. There's also a small kitchen, an office, and a laundry room with shelves for blankets. Upstairs is divided for hay and shavings. They're dropped down from chutes at each end.

"I have a two horse trailer, Emma," Luke continued. "If you'd ever like to bring Joy here for a weekend—for a little break—there's plenty of room. She might appreciate all the space. The horses enjoy swimming in the pond in the summer."

"She'd love it!" Actually, I had been thinking the same thing. I put one arm around his back, and hugged him to me. "Neither of us is thrilled with the show barn atmosphere, truth be told. But I need a trainer to help me with her."

"I've had an idea about that as well," he said, clearly nervous. "I've been considering the possibility of putting up an indoor arena. I have a friend who's a builder—we've worked on a number of projects together. I have the plans in the office. We'd attach the indoor to the barn, in a T shape, and it would look the same on the outside. White clapboard with a real roof—no noisy metal—and insulation. Windows with screens, and ceiling fans. I just have to convince the town that I'm not putting in a riding academy, and they'll approve it. I have the acreage, and the set backs are more than fine."

"Are you thinking of bringing in boarders?" I asked.

"Yes, but I can't have an in-house trainer."

"Town regs."

"Correct. However, I hear that plenty of trainers are willing to drive in, and it would give the boarders flexibility."

"And a lot less drama," I remarked.

"Exactly."

"Well," I said, attempting to remain calm. "Let me know if you need help with your presentation. I have some experience with land use hearings."

The last part of the tour included the house.

"My family settled here in 1720," Luke said. "The building that faces the drive is the original house, hand built by my ancestors, who were Zachary's great grandfather and his son. The part of the house on the left went up when Zack's parents were married. They all farmed here for generations."

We entered the oldest part of the house first. "My brother and sister and I have renovated the place a great deal," he said. "Especially after our parents died. They were real old New England Yankees. Didn't like to spend money. I have since bought out my siblings, who both have kids. The agreement is that the farm will go to the next generation, when I no longer have need of it."

This answered several of my many questions. I stayed tuned for more information.

He showed me the modern kitchen and powder room, and the big pantry, next to the laundry room. "The library is over here," Luke said. "And the original drawing room, which I rarely use."

Upstairs there were four bedrooms—one was so small, it would only accommodate a single bed, or perhaps a crib.

Luke's room was the largest. It took up one end of the floor, with an adjoining bath. The nine over nine pane windows had views of the front fields, as well as the pond and hills behind the house. There was a fireplace, wide plank flooring, and a big mahogany four poster bed.

"The bed came over from England just before the Revolution,"

he said. "It's always been in this room. I have to special order mat-
tresses for it—it's an odd size."

I walked over to the fireplace, and gazed at the portrait which
hung there. It was a woman, aged about twenty. Her reddish
brown hair was pulled back tightly. She had an intelligent, attractive face—deep blue eyes, nose slightly large, and full lips. The
dark material of her dress was softened by the bright pink shawl
around her shoulders, the ends of which she held together with
one hand. I looked closer at that hand, and caught my breath.

There was a gold ring on her index finger. On its flat, round face
the insignia was clearly visible. It was the triquetra trinity knot.

"Hannah Gates Morrison," Luke said. "Painted in 1775. She
could be your twin sister, Emma."

We were sitting in Luke's study, on the ground floor in the
newer portion of the house. It was a man's room, with the traditional English club atmosphere—built in book shelves, brown
leather couch and chairs, heavy cherry furniture, brass lamps,
antique rugs. He went to a drawer in his desk and pulled out a file.
In it was a piece of yellowed paper, encased in plastic. He handed
it to me.

12th January 1780

My Dearest Zachary,

*I am at last free to write. At times I cry out for you—but no
one hears. I have been trapped for an age in this soul less, love less
marriage.*

*I have a secret hope—it whispers of a sweet future with you.
I yearn for a deep and passionate love, Zack. I am so powerfully
drawn to you! I ache for your love that burns me, like a fire never to*

*be extinguished. I must never lose you—or I fear that I shall cease
breathing.*

*But now I am weary of this secrecy—of our forbidden passion.
I offer you my heart, Zack. When this war is done—when you are
home—I shall do as you have asked me.*

*I pray for your safety. Remember me with the tenderest affection.
As your friend and lover, I am, as always, your*

Hannah Gates Morrison

I stared at the page until my vision began to waver. "This is
amazing Luke! How do you happen to have it?"

"Let's sit down," he suggested. "I'll get the fire going. Would
you like something to drink?"

I waited impatiently until he had handed me a glass of chardonnay, and was seated next to me.

"OK," he said. "If you don't mind, I'm going to start with my
story. Don't worry—this won't take long. I was married once for a
short time. Right after grad school. Shelly was a college classmate,
so we'd known each other for years. We lived in the city. She was
never here at the farm, except for one or two holidays. There was
no drama attached to our relationship. Perhaps it would have gone
better for us if there had been. In any event—she met someone
else, and in due course we were divorced.

"I've been hearing about Zack and Hannah for as long as I
can remember. Obviously their affair wasn't something that parents crowed about through the generations. But we've always
been aware that Zack took Hannah's portrait from Bridge Hollow
School while he was a teacher there, and it's been hanging over the
fireplace in the master bedroom ever since. As the oldest son, it
was his room.

"Growing up, Hannah became a kind of ideal for me. When I was a student at BHS, I used to come in to this room and just look at her. After my divorce, I moved back up here. Hannah was still right where I'd left her, with her warm face and her kind eyes."

He took my hand. "And suddenly, one Saturday morning at the dock, there you were. With your red brown hair pulled back, your blue eyes, and that pink jacket you wear for rowing."

"My high visibility fleece," I said, stunned.

"I'm not what you'd call a particularly spiritual person, Emma. But I admit to being pretty well blown away by the resemblance between you and Hannah. I decided to keep my cool, not knowing what your situation was. And then, that night at dinner...."

"I began talking about my Hannah dreams! That must have rocked you!"

He laughed. "That's one way of putting it! Even if you had imagined the rest of the story, there's just no other way that you could have known about her ring."

We were silent for a moment.

"Do you know what happened to her?"

He nodded. "As you know, Hannah and Zachary never got together. By the time he received her letter, she was on her way to London."

"With the husband she despised," I said sadly, understanding all too well how that must have felt.

"She didn't live much longer," Luke said. "Zack sent out inquiries after the war. She died in 1783. Her husband buried her and immediately remarried—a younger, and much wealthier woman."

"Dump and suck."

"I'm sorry?"

"It's my theory about energy vampires. They dump their bad energy and suck the good energy—leaving their victim feeling empty and sick."

"And then they move on to new prey," Luke finished. "Yes, I've known one or two of those myself."

"I'm curious Luke. Why is it that no one else knows this story?"

He grinned. "There's a bit more—and I think that you especially will appreciate the irony. The family was sworn to secrecy. Remember the little boy? Christopher Marsh? Everyone assumed that his brother William was a Tory, working for a British Loyalist newspaper in New York City."

"Yes?"

"In reality, William was a spy for General Washington. And so was his best friend—from their school days. A young lawyer who joined the army in 1779."

A light bulb appeared over my head.

"Zachary."

CHAPTER TWENTY-ONE

Victory

Personal injury was at one time my favorite area of the law. I spent the first two years of my career clerking for the civil jury judges in Bridgeport, logging hundreds of hours in the courtroom. Once I had signed on with McCook, Noles and McCook in Fairfield, however, I was relegated to handling family matters and the occasional dog bite case. When I left the firm to team up with Denise, we had kept the relations friendly.

I was in the Westport office when I got a call from Basil Noles, who was the partner in charge of the civil jury caseload. He was married to the only McCook daughter, Caroline, who was quietly referred to as 'Sybil' by the support staff.

"Just heard from Len Howman's office, Em. They were looking for you. They have a pretty serious car accident case coming up for jury selection in your neck of the woods, and Len wants you to second seat him at the trial."

I asked the politically correct question. "How do the McCooks feel about that?"

"You're no longer a partner here, so they can't claim any of the proceeds."

Enough said. "Is there a date certain?"

"Len says that he's supposed to start picking a jury the first week of March."

"Why me? Why not you, or Mr. McCook?"

"The plaintiff is an equine vet. Len says he needs you because you know the lingo, and you understand these horsie types."

If only it was so.

"Len's in court all day, but he wants you to stop by his office tonight and pick up the file. His paralegal's name is Shari. She can answer all your questions."

I called Len Howman's office at five forty-five to say that I was on my way. The receptionist informed me that Shari the paralegal had just gone to the post office and would be back by the time I arrived there.

I got off 95 at exit 18 in Westport and made a left turn on to the Post Road. Howman and Freedman, PC was located in a converted old house on one of the side streets in the center of town.

Shari was a middle aged, volley ball shaped exhibit.

"I *wish* I'd been here when you called. Dr. Branden's file *can't possibly* leave the office at this time. Medical reports are still coming in." She walked over to a cabinet, pulled out a drawer, and began fingering the file tabs. Up and down. Lovingly. Would she prefer to be alone with them?

Eventually Shari recalled my presence in the room. "Once I have everything, then you can take a look at the file."

"I see. In that case, why don't I just take a copy of the defendant's deposition?"

More fingering. "It doesn't seem to be here," she announced.

"The trial is imminent, and you don't have the defendant's depo transcript?"

"I can have it emailed to you," she said, helpfully.

"No, that's fine. When you have it printed out, I'll send someone from my office to pick it up."

A tight, phony smile appeared. Reminiscent of my mother's natural visage.

"I'll call you as soon as I have it." Another female emerged from stage right. "Oh, here's Len's secretary," Shari announced. "Grace, do you two know each other? This is Nick Bennington's *ex* wife."

Aha.

I extended my right hand. "Attorney Emma Carbury. Nice to meet you."

The aforementioned Grace, sensing friction, scurried down the corridor to sanctuary.

"Do you expect Len back shortly?"

"Oh yes. He just texted me from his car."

"Wonderful. I have a long drive back to Litchfield County. Please tell him to expect my call."

"I'll do that," she said.

Tina Rosen called me Thursday morning. "Are you sitting down Em?"

I heard the jubilance in her voice. "Good news?"

"I got a call from my good buddy Jeff Merton—Tallmadge Academy's attorney. The Board made their decision late last night. Lexie has been exonerated. Completely! She's back in class today. I just got off the phone with her parents, who are thrilled."

"Congrats Tina! You did a wonderful job in there!"

"Me?" Tina hooted. "You and your intelligence gang stole the show. I don't know what was better. Carlie with her spy cam—or the dorm monitor with her killer manual."

"My favorite was the school shrink spitting out his water while Yola the Headmistress was testifying."

"Then he gave us all a stern lecture on the seriousness of Post

Traumatic Stress Disorder. I really enjoyed watching that cruel bitch squirm in her chair," Tina replied, gleefully.

"And the look of dismay on the faces of the rest of the Board!"

"It gets better, Em. Yola's history!"

"What!"

"Oh yeah. She got the ax. She's been offered the chance to resign—less publicity for the school. They've already started the search for a new Headmistress."

"What about Lexie's application to Vanderbilt?"

"Merton is drafting a letter today, explaining the outcome of the hearing, and subject to my approval, it will be sent out tomorrow."

"Good."

"The TA Board has instituted a new policy regarding bullying. It's remarkably strict."

"Tell me."

"I'll just give you the highlights. The organization known as the Protectors and Enforcers of Tradition is hereby permanently disbanded. Any student at Tallmadge Academy who engages in bullying of any kind will be subject to an immediate hearing, and if found guilty, expelled. There is no appeal process.

"The aforementioned also applies to any staff member or employee of TA who bullies a student. Immediate hearing, suspension without pay, or termination—whatever is deemed appropriate under the circumstances.

"Bullying is defined as any behavior, whether verbal or non-verbal, physical, written, or electronic, which is calculated to induce emotional or physical discomfort of any kind in its recipient.

"All staff and students shall report any instances of bullying immediately to the Deputy Headmistress, who will immediately contact the school psychiatrist, and the parents of the parties involved.

"Any member of the staff who observes an act of bullying and does not take the aforementioned action will be subject to discipline, which may include suspension or termination."

"Staff is defined as any adult who is employed by Tallmadge Academy for Girls, including but not limited to: teachers, administration, guidance counselors, advisors, dormitory monitors, coaches, and maintenance and housekeeping."

"This is wonderful Tina! Every school should have such a tough policy."

"I've saved the best for last Em!"

"There's more?"

"Therese and her entire band of Merry Women have been expelled!"

"So Sophie was right!" Carlie cheered. "That Wiccan Threefold Law works every time!"

"Karma," Julie agreed. "Mom is always reminding me about it. That's why we're both so careful."

"Yeah," Lexie nodded. "Life's tough enough, without bringing in three times more garbage to deal with."

"How are you feeling these days Lexie?" I asked.

"Much better, thanks to all of you! My parents found me a female therapist in town, and I see her once a week—at least for now. I was allowed to re take the art history exam, and I aced it. I like my new classes," she said, "but I'm looking forward to graduation and moving on."

"Small wonder," I replied. "Well ladies, let us raise our tea cups to our brave Carlotta here. She was the impetus for great change at your school, and students from now on owe her an enormous debt of gratitude, although they will know it not."

"To Carlie!" We exclaimed, as I passed around the plate of éclairs.

The Tallmadge Board of Directors hired a new Headmistress in February. Martha Barnes, Ph.D. had been the Chair of the history department at a small college in New York State, and was scheduled to begin her new reign at TA on March first.

"Finally—someone with a brain!" Carlie remarked.

"Yes," I added. "I'm not an academic snob, but I do feel that an establishment of TA's reputation should have a leader who is more impressive than a former grade school teacher at its helm."

"Someone who can communicate on a civilized adult level, you mean?" Carlie grinned. "No hidden agendas? Behavioral boundaries set firmly in place?"

I smiled. "Something like that. Yes."

Dr. Barnes asked to see me almost immediately upon taking office. She was a tall, slender woman, about fifty-five, with short graying dark hair, and cheerful brown eyes.

"This is a pleasure Attorney Carbury!" She exclaimed, shaking my hand, and giving me a warm smile. "One semester at Tallmadge Academy, and you've managed to turn the entire school around. Your student reviews were extraordinarily good, especially for a professional with no formal training in education. I can only aspire to your level of achievement!"

"You are a very welcome change here, Dr. Barnes," I replied. "And if I may say so, long overdue."

"Yes, I've had that impression from the Chair of just about every department." She sighed. "As you know, I'm sure, from the practice of law—people are not always receptive to adjustments in their routine, even if it is desperately needed."

"You're correct."

We sat down in two comfortable arm chairs.

"I've asked you to come in because I want to talk about your plans regarding the fall semester. The Board has made it clear that they would like you to stay on and teach U.S. History. Have you made a decision?"

I took a deep breath. "I've decided to do it," I announced. "I admit that committing to an entire year was a real leap of faith for me, but seeing...."

"How much you accomplished in half a year?"

"I believe that everything happens for a reason, whether we like it, or not. So perhaps there is more good that I can do here."

"Exactly my point! Excellent. I'll inform the Board of your decision. Will you be continuing with Evidence as well?"

I nodded. "For the first semester."

Dr. Barnes relaxed in her chair, her mission complete. "By the way, I've had a long conversation with Ms. Carlie Graham. A true fireball! I'm very impressed with that young woman. I have made the suggestion that she should consider investigative journalism as a career, and she has promised me that she will think about it."

"Carlie told me. She's quite excited, and has already begun researching journalism schools in New England."

Dr. Barnes laughed. "She's certainly free to change her mind in the next few years, but in the mean time, I've made a recommendation to the advisor of the school paper to bring Carlie on as a features writer this spring."

CHAPTER TWENTY-TWO

Peaceful Warrior

The Book Club assembled in our Westport office library for the March meeting.

"*Jane Eyre* everyone!" Angela announced. "Let's get started. We've heard all about Anne and Emily. Now for the most famous of the three Brontë sisters. Emma, you're up to bat."

"Please bear in mind that this book is my all time favorite novel," I said, a little sheepish, "so if I get over enthusiastic, feel free to bang a gong, or something.

"Our main sources of information regarding the Brontë family are letters which Charlotte wrote to two friends she met at school in Roe Head, from 1831 until her death in 1855. Charlotte studied at Roe Head for a year, and later returned there to teach from 1835 to 1838. Subsequently, she worked as a governess. In her letters Charlotte wrote of the details of family life, her dissatisfaction of having to earn her living as a governess, and her concerns regarding the position of women in Victorian society.

"Charlotte was also a gifted watercolorist, and she had at one point considered art as a profession.

"As we heard at last month's meeting, Charlotte and Emily attended a boarding school in Brussels to study languages in 1842, and once again Charlotte returned to Brussels for a year of teaching, from 1843 to 1844. At that time she became emotionally attached to an instructor, Monsieur Heger, who was a married man. Such a connection is seen later in her fiction, first in *Jane Eyre*, and then in *Villette*.

"*Jane Eyre* was published under Charlotte's pen name, Currer Bell, in 1847. It was a critical and commercial success. The sole survivor of her siblings, Charlotte went on to publish two more novels—*Shirley* in 1849, and *Villette* in 1853. She married her father's curate, the Reverend Arthur Bell Nichols, in 1854, and died in pregnancy in March of 1855, just short of her fortieth birthday.

"The plot of *Jane Eyre* is surprisingly tight, given that there are five distinct sections to the novel."

"Modern fiction authors could take a lesson from Charlotte's writing style," Dottie interrupted. "I'm fed up with page after page of tedious memoirs, a new voice with every chapter, and next to no dialogue. It's easier to read legal briefs."

I grinned.

"I'll start with a brief summary of each part of the story. First, Jane's childhood as an orphan with her miserable aunt and cousins. They don't force her to sleep in a cupboard under the stairs, but bad enough. She is bullied by her cousin John—more on him later, ignored by his sisters Eliza and Georgiana, and resented and disparaged by her Aunt Reed.

"Second, her time at Lowood School. Meager food, no warm clothes or boots, colds that go unattended too long. Many of the little girls die from typhus. Death of Jane's good friend Helen Burns from TB. Please note the allusion to Charlotte Brontë's older sisters, Maria and Elizabeth, who died from exposure while at school. Mr. Brocklehurst, the sanctimonious clergyman who manages Lowood, takes 'spare the rod and spoil the child' all too literally. Apparently he is skimming funds."

"Another portrait of Reverend Brontë, perhaps?" Denise wondered.

"On the plus side, Jane has a champion in the Headmistress, Miss Temple, and after six years of study, Jane becomes a teacher herself.

"In the third part of the novel, Jane moves on to her governess position at Thornfield Hall, Edward Rochester's estate. Jane's job is to teach Rochester's ward Adèle Varens. Jane has settled into her new position for a few months when she finally meets her employer. He is moody and imperious. They have many long dialogues—which pleased Dottie, I'm sure—and Jane falls for him. Meanwhile, odd events go on in the house. Jane repeatedly hears a strange laugh. Rochester's bed is set on fire in the middle of the night. A houseguest is attacked. Rochester attempts lame explanations, but Jane is not convinced.

"Jane is summoned to her Aunt Reed's deathbed, and remains at Gateshead for a month. We learn that her cousin John, who had physically abused her when they were kids, has died—probably by his own hand. He had ruined his health and the family estate, drinking and consorting with disreputable men and women. The obvious lesson here is that one must atone. You can't escape karma."

"Another Branwell Brontë portrait," Eliot commented. "Just like Arthur Huntingdon in *The Tenant of Wildfell Hall*."

"Exactly. Meanwhile, Jane returns to Thornfield, and Rochester proposes. They are in the church, about to be married, when the wedding is stopped by a lawyer from London. Jane is told that Rochester has a wife, who is insane. She is kept at the top of the house with a nurse."

"Rochester wanted to turn Jane into his mistress," Angela remarked, "without telling her."

"Selfish bastard!" Dottie exclaimed. "She's eighteen and innocent, with a strong faith in God and morality—he's almost forty. A scandal like that would have ruined her, for life."

"Miserable unhappiness can make people behave outrageously," Denise explained. "I'm seen some amazing examples of temporary madness in my work."

"We all have," Angela agreed. "It's probably wise not to judge people."

"Jane refuses to proceed against her principles, and leaves Thornfield in the middle of the night. This brings us to the fourth part of the story—the discovery of her cousins, the Rivers family—St. John Rivers, and his sisters Diana and Mary. Jane learns that she has a real family, and that she is an heiress. She divides her twenty thousand pounds between the four of them. St. John, a cold, but pious clergyman proposes marriage. He plans to be a missionary in India. Jane is actually considering his offer, when she has a telepathic moment—Mr. Rochester is calling her name.

"In the final stage of the novel Jane returns to Thornfield, but finds only blackened ruins. Rochester's wife had set the house on fire, and jumped off the roof. In his attempt to rescue her, Rochester has lost a hand, and his sight. Jane finds him living an isolated life with a small staff at Ferndean, a manor house on a farm that he owns—about thirty miles away. They are married, and within two years he recovers enough vision in one eye to see their first born son."

"You're right, Emma," Angela said, a little quietly. "You can't run from karma."

"No," I replied, thinking of the Wiccan Threefold Law. "My research claims that you can change your destiny, but not your karma. It's a debt that must be paid."

"Before their marriage Rochester is clearly jealous of Cousin St. John, with his fair hair and Grecian profile," Denise said. "I like what he says to Jane—'Your words have delineated very prettily a graceful Apollo…. Your eyes dwell on a Vulcan, a real blacksmith, brown, broad-shouldered; and blind and lame into the bargain.' The mythological analogy is apt."

"Who wants to start with analysis of the main themes in *Jane Eyre?*" Angela asked.

"The Gothic and supernatural elements are ubiquitous," Dottie said. "Uncle Reed's ghost in the Red Room. Jane's prophetic dreams. The crazy wife is described as a vampire by her brother. Lightning splitting the chestnut tree just after Jane agrees to marry Rochester—symbolic of his future disfigurement. Telepathy between the two of them. Madness and suicide of two characters in the novel. All very atmospheric."

Denise picked up her notes. "In my opinion, this book is about passion. At its core are two people who ache for everything that life can offer. Jane moves from one home to the next, always a crusader against the pettiness, hypocrisy, and cruelty that she sees, and experiences. At the age of ten, her parting words to her hard hearted Aunt Reed are singular. 'You think I have no feelings, and that I can do without one bit of love or kindness; but I cannot live so: and you have no pity.' Jane describes the release that she feels having made this speech. 'Ere I had finished this reply, my soul began to expand, to exult, with the strangest sense of freedom, of triumph, I ever felt. It seemed as if an invisible bond had burst, and that I had struggled out into unhoped-for liberty.' I suppose a therapist would call that closure."

"A shaman would call it soul retrieval," I added.

"Jane is equally indignant," Denise continued, "when her friend Helen passively accepts bullying from teachers and fellow students.

If people are always kind and obedient to those who are cruel and unjust, the wicked people would have it all their own way: they would never feel afraid, and so they would never alter, but would grow worse

*and worse. When we are struck at without a reason,
we should strike back again very hard; I am sure we
should—so hard as to teach the person who struck us
never to do it again.*

I feel that is an extraordinary statement, given what is happening right now in twenty-first century schools."

"Charlotte Brontë was a social activist—way ahead of her time," I replied.

"I'm going to jump in here with the equally prevalent feminism theme," Eliot said. "As an adult at Thornfield, Jane expresses her need for action; that the restlessness in her nature causes her discontent and pain, because she wants to experience so much more of life than being a governess. This is one of my favorite comments in the book:

> *Women are supposed to be very calm generally: but
> women feel just as men feel; they need exercise for
> their faculties, and a field for their efforts as much
> as their brothers do; they suffer from too rigid a con-
> straint, too absolute a stagnation, precisely as men
> would suffer; and it is narrow-minded in their more
> privileged fellow-creatures to say that they ought to
> confine themselves to making puddings and knitting
> stockings, to playing on the piano and embroidering
> bags. It is thoughtless to condemn them, or laugh at
> them, if they seek to do more or learn more than cus-
> tom has pronounced necessary for their sex.*

Although she is an educated, well spoken and talented young woman, Jane is still a governess—a salaried servant without social standing. She would have been bored out of her mind in the country with only the housekeeper to speak to."

"Which leads us straight to Mr. Rochester!" Angela laughed, clinking her wine glass with mine. "When Emma and I were juniors in high school English Lit, Emma announced to the entire class that Rochester was her ideal kind of man because he wasn't afraid to tell Jane how deeply he loved her. She said that his words to Jane were so romantic that they made her cry, and that she dreamed of having a husband like that some day."

"Yeah," I replied, "and then I married Nick. A man who wouldn't know what to do with a woman if he was handed a map and a flashlight."

"Rochester is passionate," Angela continued, undeterred. "And yet he manages to be a very manly man. As strong minded and opinionated as Jane is, you never feel that he is repulsed by her intelligence, or her independence. To the contrary—he seems to be braced and intrigued by it."

I smiled to myself. I suddenly saw Luke's face.

"What are you thinking about Em?" Dottie asked.

"Jane's speech to Rochester," I lied. "Just before he proposes to her.

> *I love Thornfield: I love it, because I have lived in it a full and delightful life, momentarily at least. I have not been trampled on. I have not been petrified. I have not been buried with inferior minds, and excluded from every glimpse of communion with what is bright and energetic, and high. I have talked face to face, with what I reverence; with what I delight in, with an original, a vigorous, an expanded mind.*

For years I have visualized a marriage of equals. Two people who are best friends first, who never weary of each other." I recalled too many dinners drinking glass after glass of chardonnay, while Nick droned on about himself.

Dottie flipped to the end of *Jane Eyre*. "This is what you've been looking for, Em."

To be together is for us to be at once as free as in solitude, as gay as in company. We talk, I believe, all day long: to talk to each other is but a more animated and an audible thinking. All my confidence is bestowed on him, all his confidence is devoted to me; we are precisely suited in character—perfect concord is the result.

You're just like Jane—a peaceful warrior who stands up for people. You'll find a man who admires that in you—who really gets you."

"It seems as though he's finally here, Emma," Angela said, gently. "You just have to be open to it."

Denise and I sat in the library after everyone else had left.

"I ran into Tina Rosen in court Emma," Denise said. "She was thrilled with the way that the two of you worked together in Bridge Hollow. She said that you have quite a following of free thinkers up there."

"That was kind of her. Tina's a terrific lawyer—our kind of professional. Smart, efficient, high ethics, and compassion for the client."

"What do you think about offering her a position with us?" Denise asked.

"I think it's a great idea, if she's interested."

"No harm in asking—she's been with that old boy firm in Bridgeport for a while. She may be receptive to a change. And it would free you up to expand our satellite office in Litchfield County. With your new contacts at Tallmadge Academy, it will be easier now. That's what you want to do, isn't it Emma?"

"It is. The drive back and forth is a bit much, I have to admit."

"And now there's Luke."

I grinned. "Yes. That too."

"Tina says that he's very attractive, and obviously crazy about you."

I felt my face turn red.

Denise laughed. "I can't wait to meet him!"

Joanne had the week off, so Meredith, the owner of Apple Ridge, had coerced me into my first lesson with Frank Shaw, the jumper trainer.

Professional riders are generally intolerable. Not the amateurs, who show for pleasure. Not the grooms, who are usually committed to excellent care. The men and women who train and show and sell horses for a living. They are arrogant and condescending, backstabbing and vindictive. They consider horses to be little more than used cars, and their websites reflect this attitude. They are doing you a big favor by conducting business with you. It is all about the money, and their status in the big league.

Occasionally, I had come across a real gem; the true horse person. A trainer who worked for the love of the animals and with a genuine desire to help clients improve.

Five minutes into my lesson, I had Frank pegged as a member of the first category.

"I heard that Joy has shown in the high preliminaries, and some modified open classes," he remarked. "Joanne says that she's very talented."

"Yes."

"That Joy's won some impressive ribbons at big shows."

"Correct."

"But now you want to turn her into an amateur horse?"

"I want to be able to ride her very well. That's my goal."

"She's difficult, right?"

"Joy is opinionated, certainly."

"You haven't been riding very long?"

"About five years."

"I would never have matched an advanced jumper with a relatively new rider. You should sell her and buy a nice seasoned gelding. An older guy who will pack you around the ring. I could get you a good price each way. Joy still has a lot of jumps left in her."

I didn't bother to respond. Frank was clearly calculating his sales commissions as he spoke.

"Then we could get you in the show ring right away."

"Joy is a member of my family and I have no intention of selling her."

"Joanne told me. But as your professional, I...."

"I'm a *licensed* professional. Joy stays with me." I summarily determined that our lesson was over.

Gloria, the barn manager, found me in the tack room.

"Frank just told me that you're impossible to work with. What happened?"

"A total stranger just tried to manipulate me into making him some money by selling my horse and finding me a replacement," I replied, temper barely in check.

Gloria lowered her voice. "Be careful, Emma. Frank is really tight with Meredith, and you know that Meredith carries Rob's penis around in her purse. If she decides that she wants you out of this barn, Rob will cave immediately."

"Even if it means losing a good client?"

"Rob doesn't care about clients!" Gloria whispered fiercely. "He cares about keeping Meredith happy, because when she's happy, she's quiet. And she pays the bills around here." Gloria paused. "This isn't Fairfield County, Emma. If you need a trainer and an indoor, there aren't a lot of options. Better to keep your head down, and play the game."

"What a pathetic way to do business."

"That's horse people for you."

I stopped at Bridge Hollow Tack to pick up Joy's new Rambo turn out. Lindsay handed me the big shopping bag.

"I finally found out why Frank Shaw left Melanie's farm," she informed me. "Several dissatisfied clients now board their horses at various other locations, and were eager to relate the story."

Ah yes. Lack of discretion in the horse show world was rampant.

"It seems that Frank had created his own little war zone at Mel's," Lindsay continued. "He quietly backstabbed each client to the others, leading each woman to believe that she was his favorite student, and that her particular horse was the most talented in the barn. This tactic kept the ladies competitive, jealous, and down right bitchy toward each other."

"But loyal to Frank, who appeared to be neutral." I had seen this divide and conquer strategy work in law firms as well. "Was he sleeping with any of them?"

Lindsay shook her head. "Not to my knowledge. My sources say that it was merely the unspoken promise of intimacy which had these women race to bring Frank his first cup of coffee in the morning, take him out to dinner, even buy him gifts." Lindsay wrinkled her nose. "I don't get it," she said. "The guy seems like such a phony slime ball to me."

"Weak minded people need someone to worship, Lindsay. So how did the situation finally blow up?"

"Frank misjudged the intelligence of a new client, who's a financial consultant with Wall Street experience, and used to dealing with men who get off on head fucks. Apparently Frank began mouthing off about Susan's horse, how Diamond wasn't talented enough, and Susan wasn't competent to ride him."

"Let me guess," I broke in. "Frank offered to find her a wonderful new hunter, and a buyer for Diamond at the same time."

"Of course," Lindsay replied. "We've all been victims of that line of garbage, right? Well, Susan went straight to Mel and complained. Mel started speaking to the other clients, and Frank was out. He'd been catch riding for a while, and now he's snookered Meredith at your barn."

"Great."

"Melanie has a new trainer, and everyone's happy. No indoor though, which as you know, is a big problem in the winter, especially up here."

"Yes. A big problem. Thanks Lindsay."

"You're welcome. Just watch your back. Joy's exactly the kind of jumper that Frank needs to give his career a leg up."

CHAPTER TWENTY-THREE

Jury Selection

I met Len Howman at Litchfield Superior Court promptly at nine o'clock.

"OK, Emma, what kind of juror do we want?"

"The kind that's been in lots of car accidents and goes to the chiropractor every day?"

"Exactly right," he said, maneuvering his file trolley through the metal detector. "Judge Wolfe is holding a conference before we begin. I want you to do most of the talking."

The Honorable Harold Wolfe was an enormous bulk of man. An ex Marine, his bald head and gruff manner induced every lawyer in front of him to wish that his or her shoes were shined to a higher standard of gleam. I checked my own navy heels as we followed the clerk into the inner sanctum.

The judge trained his sights on counsel for the defense. "Your adjustor here yet, Vinnie?"

"Yeah, Judge, he's in the courtroom."

My turn. "Your client here, Ms. Carbury?"

"Same, your honor."

"Good. How far apart are you people?"

Vincent Pellicione pulled out a file. "The plaintiff is claiming a thirty percent permanent partial disability rating, with injuries to his back, neck, and left arm."

"I can read the complaint, counselor. I want numbers."

"Mr. Howman filed an offer of judgment three years ago for eight hundred thousand, your honor," I answered.

"The insurance company will pay two fifty to make the case go away," Pellicione replied.

"The plaintiff is an equine veterinarian who works primarily with breeding farms. He will probably be on pain killers for the rest of his life, and may require back surgery in the near future."

"There's no question of liability, right?"

"None, your honor. My client was stopped at an intersection. The defendant lost control of his truck and struck him broadside."

"So we're going to have a hearing in damages?"

"Correct, your honor."

The judge flipped through the file. "I want you to talk to that adjustor again, Vinnie. We've got huge medical bills here, lost wages, damage to the car, future pain and suffering. Your people could get hit much harder than eight hundred grand. Otherwise, we're going to start jury selection in half an hour."

Vinnie went back out into the courtroom.

"What's doing Len? How's your golf?" The men conducted their old boy club meeting. I read through my questions for the potential jurors.

Vinnie reappeared. "He's willing to come up another fifty thousand, Judge."

The Honorable Wolfe put on his robe. "Tell the jury clerk that we're ready to come in," he said to his courtroom clerk. "I'm going to sit in on this. Maybe it will move quicker."

Len and I repaired to the courtroom to collect our client. "We're gonna start, Kevin," Len said to Dr. Branden. "First, we all file into the jury assembly room, and the panel is sworn in by the clerk. The judge informs today's gathering about the case, and then each lawyer goes to the microphone and tells the group about their firms and who they will call as witnesses. Then the judge asks if there are any conflicts. After that, we move back into the courtroom, and we interview the panelists, one by one. You'll sit with us at counsel table. We'll consult you before we accept or excuse any juror."

"I don't ask them questions, do I?"

"Nope. That's Emma's job."

"What happens if we don't like one of them?"

"We only get four peremptory challenges," I replied. "They're discretionary, which means that we don't have to give our reasons for excusing the person. However, as we need six jurors and two alternates, we must be very careful how we use our discards. The good news is that we're allowed unlimited challenges for cause."

"What are they?"

"If the potential juror gives an answer that is clearly biased for or against one side, then the judge will step in and ask questions. He may then excuse the person himself."

Fifteen minutes later, our first *voir dire* contestant walked into the jury box, sat down, and looked up at me expectantly. Not unlike Abby, just before dinner.

I approached the jury box. I had already perused this woman's questionnaire in our packet. "Good morning, Mrs. Seldes. I see that you have been a registered nurse for twenty years."

"That's correct."

"Do you practice in a specific area of medicine?"

"I've worked in the critical care ward for the last five years."

"Do you deal with many car accident cases on your floor?"

"No. They go to the trauma center."

"Have you ever been in a car accident?"

"Two or three fender benders."

"Did you sustain any injuries from those accidents?"

"No."

"Has anyone in your family ever been in a car accident?"

"No."

"Do you have any problems with your back?"

"Sometimes, if I sit for too long."

"Is this the result of an injury?"

"No. It's the result of old age."

"Would you have any problem with sitting on this case? Would it be uncomfortable for you?"

"No, I don't think so."

"What about your neck? Any problems?"

"No."

"Either of your arms?"

"No."

"Have you ever been treated by a chiropractor?"

"No."

"Is there any reason why you wouldn't consider being treated by a chiropractor?"

"No."

"Have you or any member of your family ever owned a horse?"

"No."

"Any experience with horses? You, or your family?"

"No."

"Can you think of any reason why you could not be a fair and impartial juror in this case?"

"No."

"Thank you Mrs. Seldes. Mr. Pellicione has some questions."

I sat down. Len passed me a note: "A little cold, but we should take her." I nodded.

Vinnie started to pace around the area in front of the judge's bench. "Do you read any magazines, Mrs. Seldes?"

"Nursing journals, mostly."

"Do you have any hobbies?"

"I do some gardening. I like to cook. That's about it."

"What about sports?"

"No."

"Do you own any pets?"

"We have a cat."

"Do you have a regular veterinarian?"

"Yes."

"Do you see the vet often?"

"No. Just the annual shots, usually."

"Thank you Mrs. Seldes. I have nothing further."

The marshal escorted Mrs. Seldes out in to the hall and closed the door.

"Accepted, your honor," I reported.

"Excused," Vinnie announced. I sighed inwardly. This was going to take a long time.

By the end of business on Tuesday, we had six jurors. The judge brought us into chambers at four forty-five, for a last minute hounding.

"I expect to be ready to start evidence on Thursday morning, counselors. Everybody got their experts lined up?"

"Yes, your honor," I said.

"Yeah, Judge," Vinnie replied. "My guy is coming down from Harvard on Friday."

"He's an opinion witness, correct? Not a treating physician?"

"That's right, Judge."

Len and I looked at each other. Juries tended to frown on physicians who were hired guns.

"So, we'll have our two alternates tomorrow, right counselors?"

"Absolutely Judge. No problem," Vinnie replied, loosening his tie.

"I want requests to charge from both sides before you leave tomorrow. Clear?"

"Yes, your honor."

"Sure Judge."

"And I want all of the exhibits pre marked by the clerk."

"Already done, your honor."

"Good. I'll see you all on the dot of nine thirty tomorrow morning."

"Think your trial will settle?" Carlie asked.

"It would be great if it did. We have some concerns about the scene of the accident photos."

"How come? I thought you said that the pictures were really gross and the jury would love them."

"They would. The photos are awful. The problem is, we just found out who took them."

"OK. So who?"

"Our client."

"Uh, the horse doc who's supposed to be so mashed up? He just happened to have a camera?"

"He always has one with him, he said."

"To take pictures of baby horses?"

"No. To record any UFO sightings that he happens to make."

Carlie burst out laughing. "That's some job you have!"

"Yeah, I know. And I could really do with a vacation. Your spring break is coming up. Want to come along?"

"Sure. Where are we going?"

"Paris."

After several weeks of rain we were finally able to ride in the outdoor on Sunday.

"Be careful," Joanne had warned. "The horses may be a little crazy from being in their stalls for so long."

But they were perfect angels. Joy and I stood by the rail, watching Canadian geese in the pond. One of them suddenly flapped its huge wings and took flight. The others followed suit, squawking loudly in concert. They flew over our heads, casting a dark shadow on the left half of the ring. Joy twitched one ear. A breeze caught her mane and ruffled it. She sighed, a picture of contentment.

"I noticed that the horse show sign-up sheets have been posted," Becky said to Gloria.

"We're doing the usual A circuit shows this year, including HITS, and three weeks in Manchester. Meredith wants to know who's interested, so she can book stalls."

"What is Joy doing this summer, Emma?" Hallie asked.

"Well, since I have no interest in showing, Joanne is talking about doing some dressage tests with her."

"So no more jumping?" Gloria asked, looking confused. "Does Frank know that? I heard him talking about taking Joy to the Turner Farm hunter/jumper show. It's a big, rated event."

"Really?" I replied, that dangerous tone in my voice. "Then he made the decision without discussing it with me."

Frank and Meredith walked out of the barn together with one of Meredith's fancy hunters. Gloria immediately moved away from us.

"What's going on with her?" Becky asked, watching Gloria ride off.

"Either she didn't want to appear to be gossiping with the clients, or she didn't want to be spoken to about loafing. Take your pick," Hallie said.

"We need a check from you for stalls at Saratoga, Hallie,"

Meredith announced breezily, as she moved her horse to the mounting block. "You and your daughter are both going, right?"

Hallie flushed. "Just Lynn."

"I like to have everything set and organized early. What about you Becky?"

"This week."

Meredith turned to me. "Joy's fees for Turner Farm are due now, Emma."

"Joy's not showing in the jumpers this season," I replied.

Meredith's face turned to stone. "Frank wants to ride her in the high prelims."

I'll bet he did.

"Joanne will be taking her to a few dressage tests. That's it."

"Frank is the head trainer here. He runs the program."

Frank's expression was smug.

"Joy is my horse," I responded, my voice firm. "Any final decision regarding Joy ends with me. I want Joanne to ride her."

"I'm going to have to speak to Rob about this." Meredith moved off at the trot, posting on the wrong diagonal.

"Frank just wants the ribbons that he knows he'll get with Joy," Becky whispered.

"He won't get any ribbons if Joy decides to kill him first." I steered Joy over to the gate and dismounted.

Luke and I met for lunch later that week. The topic for discussion was our mutual birthdays, which were eight days apart. I apologized that Carlie's spring break coincided with that particular week, and that we would be in Paris. Luke and I agreed to celebrate upon my return.

"You *do* realize that we were both born under the sign of Aries, don't you?" I asked him, laughing. His birthday was March thirtieth. Mine was April seventh.

"I didn't know that you were into astrology, as well as witchcraft and shamanism," he replied.

"I'm not," I grinned, throwing a sweet potato fry at him. "But Sophie is. She wanted me to tell you that we have our work cut out for us. Aries is ruled by the planet Mars, apparently, who was the Roman god of war. It's a fire sign…."

"I'll grant you the fire."

"And our symbol is the ram. You know—curly horns clashing and locking?"

"On barren, snow covered peaks? Got it."

"Aries men and women are known for their leadership abilities, as well as for their courage and physical energy."

"That certainly fits," Luke said, drily. There was a pause.

"How's Joy?" He asked. "Any new drama at your barn?"

I smirked. "The owner's wife, Meredith, better known as She Who Has the Cash, is a consistent pain in the ass. No one can stand her, but Apple Ridge is the best farm around, and none of the boarders feel like spending an hour or more in the car round trip to see our horses. So we nod and smile, and kiss her butt, regardless of how outrageously she behaves."

"What's she up to now?"

"Just more of same, I guess. Meredith takes over whenever she's in the ring, working with Frank to perfect her look for showing in the hunters. If she's jumping, and she always is, the rest of us are crowded into a corner until she's done, even if we're in the middle of a lesson. Which we pay her for. She's loud and opinionated, and feels free to toss evil remarks at anyone, whenever she feels like it, because she's the boss. We're all braced and wincing from her abuse, most of the time."

"Sounds like this Meredith has got you all under her thumb."

"Unfortunately. The best part is watching her flirt with Frank, the head trainer. He's obviously giving her regular lube jobs, and her husband Rob doesn't seem to have a clue."

"Or doesn't care."

"You're probably right. Meredith lives off her trust fund and has her husband twirled around her ring finger. Rob has two priorities: keeping Meredith happy, and selling horses." I took a bite of my chopped salad. "And Meredith likes Frank. So, you can imagine how much weight a boarder's concerns about Frank will have with Rob."

"What's Frank's story?"

"His teaching style is a delightful combination of cajole and torture, and you never know what day it is. His students are always out of control in the ring, and the horses roar around the jumps wild eyed and lathered in sweat. None of us will work in the same area with him, which is tough if the weather's bad, and the only option is the indoor."

Luke shook his head. "But you and Joy are staying put?"

"For now. At least Meredith and Frank are away a lot, showing, so we get some reprieve. Joy and I love Joanne. The care is terrific and the facility is beautiful. What's that quotation? Something like 'where every prospect pleases, and only man is vile'?"

"That pretty much covers all of Western Connecticut."

CHAPTER TWENTY-FOUR

Napoleon

Postcard to Angela, a view of Pont Neuf and the Ile de la Cité from the Right Bank:

> Hi Ange,
>   The stunning beauty of this city! This is my second visit, yet I still feel completely overwhelmed by it all. The history, the elegance, the total ambiance of being in the most sophisticated place on earth. We just had a wonderful meal at a café near the Eiffel Tower, which included a hefty dollop of chocolate mousse. We're staying in a hotel in the Luxembourg Quarter, near the garden, and an easy walk to the river. Jet lag is still bad, but we will persevere. We're climbing the Tower tonight.
>   Love, Emma

Postcard from Carlie to Julie, view of Napoleon's head on a gold coin:

Hey Jules!

The flight turned out to be not so bad after all—Emma flirted with some guy at the desk, and we got upgraded to business class. The Parisians so far seem pretty nice, but part of that may be the cleavage that Emma is showing everywhere we go. We took the elevator to the top of the Eiffel Tower last night. Emma had to be drunk to do it, and when they turned on the strobe lights, I thought she was going to be sick. Food's great! And OMG! the hot guys!!!   Luv ya, Carlie

Email to Sophie entitled: "Up to here with World War Two."

Dear Sophie,

Carlie is working on a huge paper for her European history class, so we spent the afternoon with General de Gaulle et al in the Musée de l'Armée. The nineteen thirties and forties from the French perspective. The way they tell it, the entire war was fought by their Underground Resistance people, and the Americans and Brits were nowhere near Paris when it was finally liberated from the Germans in 1944.

Also worth noting: plenty of Japanese tourists in this museum, which became quite interesting when we got to the Pacific theatre exhibit.

We also viewed the gallery devoted to Napoleon. I was especially entranced with his stuffed horse (more like a pony, really) and his stuffed dog. Also his death mask. Heard one French mother explain to her small son that

Napoleon was not considered a hero by everyone in the world. Considering how his career ended, I felt this to be a startling example of understatement.

We visited the Emperor's tomb, in the Dôme Church of the Hôtel des Invalides. Huge hunk of reddish stone, but no mention of his name. Just Napoleon's victories, in a circle on the floor.

As a form of relief, Carlie has agreed to tolerate a bus tour to Giverny with me tomorrow afternoon. I need a good dose of Monet after three hours of war and dead things.

All best, Emma

Postcard from Carlie to her sister Jackie at UVM, portrait of Marie-Antoinette in the Conciergerie, awaiting her execution at the guillotine:

Ma chère soeur Jacqueline! We stayed down by the Seine all day, and then walked around the islands and toured Notre-Dame while a mass was in session. There were signs everywhere begging people to be quiet, but idiots babbled loudly anyway. Spooky place. Had lunch by a little riverside stall, where they squash ham and cheese in a waffle iron thing. Pretty good. Emma wanted to look at the inside of Sainte-Chapelle, but I talked her out of it. Enough with the churches! The rose window looked fine from the outside.   XO Carlie

Postcard to Denise, view of the Left Bank, with *les bouquinistes* in the foreground:

Dear Denise,

This morning we took the Metro to Montmartre and climbed the hill to Sacré-Coeur. It sits overlooking the city, rather more like a mosque than a church. The usual throng of vendors tried to sell us things, but worth it for the unbelievable panoramic views of the city. Montmartre is a little too honky-tonk for my taste, but we saw the Moulin Rouge and a sign advertising the Erotica Museum. Carlie was enthralled. We're leaving in a bit for a bus trip to Giverny.

Best, Emma

Postcard to Luke, view of Monet's *Impression: Sunrise* (1872):

Today was our trip to Giverny to see chez Monet. The Japanese water garden was amazing—masses of interesting plantings along the banks, and the reflections on the water were always changing. Wisteria was growing all over the bridge. We heard that light through the cherry blossoms is especially dramatic. The French garden in front of the house will be glorious in a few months—arbors of roses, huge purple allium, and scented lilies. I could paint here for weeks. Carlie says that she's learned way too much about gardening on this trip. Wish you were here with us—Emma.

"Nice touch," Carlie remarked, reading over my shoulder. "Not too gushy, but sweet all the same. And lots about flowers. Luke will like that."

"I feel guilty for being away for his birthday," I admitted.

"It's your birthday too, though," Carlie said, practically. "And you two aren't at the week in Paris stage yet."

"No."

"What's the matter?" Carlie asked, with one eye on the menu. We'd opted for a civilized breakfast at a café near our hotel.

"I was just thinking that this is my fourth trip to this country, and I have yet to experience any romance."

"That's pathetic!" Carlie exclaimed.

"If you're hungry," I retorted, "I recommend the *petit déjeuner Anglais*. It's eggs and bacon with a quarter baguette, a croissant, coffee, and juice."

"Wow, these people eat bread with everything. *And* a croissant?"

"Wrap it in your napkin and save it for later," I advised.

"Look at that couple over there," Carlie remarked. I attempted that slow turn of the head that never fooled anyone. Two tables to my right sat the textbook example of a Parisian couple. He was conducting some pretty serious Public Display of Affection on Her upper body, while She entertained herself by observing us with disdain.

"He's so good looking!" Carlie whispered fiercely. "And she looks like a horse." Mr. Casually Sexy was an obvious foil to his partner's severe dark suit and tightly wound scarf.

"And what's with the scarves in this city?" Carlie demanded, too loudly. "They wear them with everything!"

We watched as Miss Sophistication smirked, while her companion never even paused the sucking action on her cheek.

"Why don't we discuss our agenda for the day?" I replied. "*Quietly.*"

We agreed to begin with the Arc de Triomphe and proceed from there.

In 1806, the Emperor Napoleon decreed that a triumphal arch in the Roman style was to be erected to the glory of his Grand Armée. After he divorced his wife, the Empress Josephine, who had failed to exercise her womanly duty and bear him an heir, he married Marie-Louise of Austria in 1810. The Arc was to be part of the procession to their wedding at the Louvre. However, Napoleon was not in power long enough to see his vision come to fruition. The Arc was eventually finished in 1836. It is located on a circle which radiates into twelve points of major arteries, the most well known being the Champs-Elysées.

Driving in the area is what the Parisians call a 'challenge.' We descended into the tunnel, walked underneath the huge traffic circle, and emerged on the street level near the Tomb of the Unknown Soldier. We climbed the long spiral staircase to the top of the Arc. One reaches first an attic story, which houses an enclosed museum, and then more stairs to the open terrace at the top. Granted, I was not properly shod, but it was a while before my breathing became even remotely normal.

The views, however, were phenomenal. Before us, in every direction, stretched the tree-lined expanses of some of the most famous avenues in the world.

We shopped first at Hermès.

"*Parlez-vous anglais?*" I asked politely of the exquisitely dressed young woman at the scarf counter. "*Un peu,*" she replied, with an embarrassed smile. We spent an agreeable twenty minutes communicating in French and hand gestures, while we picked out gorgeous squares of silk for myself and Carlie.

"I totally like this dark pink one with the ruffled edge," Carlie said. Her face lit up as the woman tied it around her neck. Carlie twirled in the mirror with her chin up.

I laughed. "I thought you were anti scarf."

"Not when they're this gorgeous!" Carlie exclaimed. "I'm open to exploring new cultures. This is supposed to be an educational trip for me!"

We strolled by famous jewelry stores and couture houses. We stepped into Chanel and fulfilled some cosmetic requirements.

We walked by a lingerie boutique—*Martine*, and I stopped.

"Want to check it out?" Carlie asked brightly.

Inside were gorgeous displays of true Parisian romance. I walked over to a peignoir that was hanging on its own from a brass fixture. It was the classic two piece combing gown—floor length spaghetti strap negligée with matching long sleeved robe in French vanilla silk, embroidered with tiny bunches of lavender in delicate purples and greens. Cream colored lace edged the bodices, and the sleeve cuffs. The robe closed with small mother of pearl buttons.

I checked the tag. Size 44. "That is size 12 in American," the sales woman said.

"Your size!" Carlie announced. "So it was meant to be. Go try it on."

Of course it was perfect. I bought elegant heeled slippers to match.

We debriefed at the hotel during cocktail hour.

"Let's go over what we did today, so you can email your parents."

"We walked through some garden with fountains."

"The Jardin des Tuileries."

"And then we did the Louvre. The glass pyramid was pretty amazing, really," she said. "My favorite piece was the Venus de Milo."

"Mine is still Winged Victory," I said. "What did you think of the Mona Lisa?"

"A little small—I was kind of disappointed," she replied. "Good timing, though. We just got in ahead of several bus loads of tourists."

"My favorite section of the museum is the European paintings." I remarked. "I liked that there were artists set up with easels in the corridors, copying famous pictures. They must have been students—I don't think I've ever seen that in the big museums back home. It's really difficult to make art with strangers hanging over your shoulder all the time."

"I noticed that when we were on the river," Carlie said. "People were really obnoxious. They came right up behind us."

"The students at the Louvre seemed to choose Renaissance paintings," I continued, thoughtfully. "I have never understood the appeal of those nasty little *putti,* with their ugly faces and fat, naked limbs. I would have chosen one of the English landscapes to copy, or even a still life."

"Face it, Emma," Carlie said, popping an *hors-d'oeuvre* into her mouth. "You just don't like little kids."

Carlie announced that she wanted to sleep in the next morning. I decided to paint. I walked by the beautiful Jardin du Luxembourg, north on Boulevard Saint Michel, toward the Seine. At the River, I turned right, passed the Place du Petit Pont, and found an empty bench on the Pont au Double. To my left was the stupendous Notre-Dame cathedral on the larger island— Ile de la Cité. Directly in front of me, the Pont de L'archevéché, with Ile St-Louis beyond. The weather, which had been chilly and overcast with bouts of light rain for most of our trip, had suddenly changed. After days of watching residents stroll by in dark pants and short, tightly belted raincoats, Parisian women were emerging in pretty spring dresses. I had chosen a particularly daring, sky blue number myself, with more than my usual allotment of décolleté. I pulled down my rose colored shades and studied my subject.

I painted a cerulean blue sky with wisps of white clouds, and a slightly grayer tone for the river. I drew the stones that paved the sheer sides of the tiny island, and then covered them with a light wash of raw umber, with Payne's gray for shadows and a little burnt sienna in the foreground. I mixed a warm and a cool color to paint the greenery that hung down the stonework to the water, and I used a minute, size one brush to do the lamp posts, the grill work on the next bridge, and the intricate windows on the western end of the cathedral in sepia. The railings on the Pont au Double were a strong copper color. I applied more burn sienna with a little red to bring it forward in the composition.

"You have forgotten the boat rings."

A tall—and I must say, extremely good looking—member of the *gendarmerie* was leaning over my shoulder, obviously more attracted to my cleavage than my sketchbook.

"You're right, I have," I replied, shockingly flirtatious. "How did you know to speak English?"

"You see, your guide book is right here," he said, practically.

"So it is."

"Where are you from?"

"Connecticut." He looked blank. "It's the little square that sticks into New York."

"Ah yes. Are you near to Yale?"

I laughed. "About an hour and a half north. Do you know someone who went to school there?"

"Just several of your Presidents," he grinned. "Not personally, you understand." He indicated my belongings displayed beside me on the bench. "May I have your camera? You should have a picture of yourself painting on such a beautiful day."

I handed over my little 35 mm. "That would be very kind of you." He took shots from several different angles, including one from behind me. Passersby stopped, clearly amused. I tried to imagine a member of the NYPD behaving as he did, and failed.

"I hope you have an enjoyable stay in Paris," the nice policeman said finally, handing back my camera.

"It's been wonderful so far," I replied. "This has got to be the most glorious city in the world."

How else could a true Parisian respond? "Oh, *absolument*," he said.

When I returned to our suite, Carlie was dressed, and enthusiastic about lunch.

"I want one of those burgers with the fried egg on top," Carlie announced. "They're weird looking, but tasty."

After lunch, we regrouped by the *grand basin* in the Jardin du Luxembourg. Three small boys were sailing their mini yachts in the octagonal pond.

"Well?" Carlie, the action teen, was ready to be on the move again. "What are we going to do with the rest of our day?"

"We should take a boat ride on the Seine," I suggested, "so you'll feel more oriented. We'll go by the Eiffel Tower, the Louvre, the Musée d'Orsay, the islands, the famous bridges. It takes about an hour. Then we can plan future adventures."

"Please explain to me why there is a mini Statue of Liberty in the middle of the Seine," Carlie asked, pointing.

"According to my guide book, this replica was given to the French people by the American community in Paris. It is one third the size of the one in New York, and stands on the man-made Ile aux Cygnes, near Pont de Grenelle, in the Seine. This Liberty faces west toward the Atlantic, and New York. The statue was dedicated on July 4, 1889, and the tablet bears two dates—July 4, 1776, and July 14, 1789—the storming of the Bastille, which triggered the French Revolution.

"The figure is Libertas, the Roman goddess of freedom. The

American statue stands on Liberty Island in New York Harbor. She was a gift from the people of France in 1886. At her feet is a broken chain, and the tablet commemorates the signing of the Declaration of Independence, on July 4, 1776."

"Did our Revolution spark theirs?"

"*Mais bien sûr, chérie!*" I replied. "The Marquis de Lafayette was 'the hero of two worlds.' You should have learned that in European history."

Two hours later, we crossed to the Right Bank on the Pont d'Iéna.

The Chaillot hill was originally designated by Napoleon as the site of a grand palace for his son. However, the Emperor's reign did not last long enough to build it. The Place du Trocadéro was created in 1878. It is overlooked by the Palais du Chaillot, which was constructed for the World Fair of 1937. It is a massive structure, designed in the Neoclassical style, with two curved wings. It houses several museums and a cultural center. I wasn't impressed with the modern palace, but the view was incomparable. From the terrace in front of the Palais, the vista is of the Jardins du Trocadéro with the fountains in the foreground, down to the Seine, and the Eiffel Tower on the other side of the river.

"Napoleon sure liked building monuments to himself, huh?" Carlie noted.

"Question," I began, putting down my camera, and taking out my guidebook. "What is the difference between a leader and a bully?"

"Your point is?"

"OK, I'll be a bit more clear. What's the difference between a leader and a dictator?"

"Um, one brings out the best in people with wisdom—the other tortures them into submission?"

I was stunned. "That's pretty astute Carlotta."

"Well, we've been talking about this in class. There's a difference between liberty and power. It seems like the countries that have made it—stayed intact—have been the ones that went the democratic route. Even the Brits—they've had a constitutional monarchy for centuries. It works for them. The places with whackos at the top—like Germany and Italy, or the Middle East—haven't done so well."

"And France?"

"Mr. Sutton says that Americans should always be grateful to the French, because we never would have won the Revolution without them. Benjamin Franklin signed the alliance treaty here in France in 1778, and then the Treaty of Paris in 1783, which ended the war."

"Let's talk about a real leader—look at General Washington," I said. "When our Revolution was over, he resigned his commission as Commander-in-Chief to the Continental Congress. Did you know that there was talk of making him King George I of America? Instead, he went home to Mount Vernon, where he stayed until he was called back to Philadelphia to serve as president of the Constitutional Convention in 1787. Washington was known as the father of our country—famous everywhere! He could have taken advantage of that, really thrown his weight around, but he never did. He let the country decide. Then in 1789, he became our first President." I paused. "Now. Think about Napoleon."

"The soldier turned Emperor?"

"Yes! He was the most brilliant general in the French army. But after their Revolution, Napoleon crowned himself and his wife in 1804, and proceeded to fight war after war until he was defeated by Wellington at Waterloo. He died in exile in 1821."

I handed her the book.

"So the moral is what? Acting humble will get you everywhere?"

"Partially, yes. The main point is that you can't give lip service to liberty, Carlie. Liberty, equality, fraternity. You're either serious about it—committed to it—or you're going to get it in the neck. The French aristocrats learned that the hard way."

"Karma again, huh?"

"The Threefold Law of the Universe."

Carlie settled herself on the steps to write postcards. I started to sketch the Eiffel Tower. Suddenly the fountains began to play. I hurried forward with my camera. The sprays were operated in sequence; the finale was the firing of the huge water cannon in the center. This scene was probably one of the most famous portraits of the city of Paris—a night time view of the illuminated fountains shooting water toward the Eiffel Tower, which in turn is sparkling with flashing lights.

I was determined to return to Paris soon. When Luke and I were ready.

CHAPTER TWENTY-FIVE

Venus and Mars

I was in my bedroom when I heard Luke's car pull up. I checked the mirror on my dressing table one last time. My Parisian peignoir was beautiful. The cream colored lace and the embroidered lavender brought out the deep blue in my eyes.

I opened the front door. His smile changed immediately to surprise.

"I take it that dinner is postponed, then?" He asked gently, stepping inside and closing the door.

"Dinner," I replied, taking the bottle of wine from him, and placing it on the table behind me, "is *definitely* postponed."

When I emerged from the shower on Saturday morning, Luke was bending over my dressing table, attempting to comb his hair in the mirror. Abby was stretched out on the bed, watching him.

"There's another bathroom down the hall," I said, laughing. His six foot three frame looked incongruous amongst the crystal perfume bottles and pink candles.

"Good to know," he said.

More kissing and hugging. I could get used to this.

"Do you have any coffee?" Luke asked. "For some reason, I'm having trouble waking up."

"Hi-test French roast," I replied, leading him down to the kitchen. "If you don't mind helping yourself, I will address Abby's needs." I opened the back door to let her out, and then filled her food and water dishes. "There are pastries from Isabella's on the counter," I said, indicating the white box.

We took our breakfast out to the porch and sat watching Abby taunt some chipmunks by the dock. The sky was that crisp cloudless blue of early spring. The lake was still as glass.

"Emma," Luke said, taking my hand. "What are you looking for, if anything, in a relationship?"

I'd been thinking about this since we'd met. "I want a best friend, Luke. I want to have fun, I want to have adventures. But most of all, I want someone who I *know* will watch my back. I need to feel safe."

He sat looking at me for a bit. "Safe." It wasn't a question. He just seemed to be processing the concept. "With someone as sure and true as you are."

Amazing man. "Yes. Exactly. Otherwise, frankly—I'd rather spend the rest of my life alone." My voice was harsher than I'd intended, but Luke didn't appear to mind.

"I see," he said, slowly. "What will convince you, do you think?"

"Time," I replied, firmly. "Give and take. Space, when I need it," I added.

I took a little box out of my pocket. "Happy Birthday, Luke. I'm sorry that I was away for the actual day, but I hope that this will make up for it."

He opened the box. Inside I had placed a key.

"It's the front door," I said quickly. "I also have a garage remote for you. I'd like to keep the neighborly gossip down to a minimum."

"Thanks." His head was still bent over the box.

"Is it OK?" I asked nervously. "Or too soon, do you think?"

"Perfect timing," he said. He suddenly got to his feet, pulled me out of my chair, and started waltzing with me on the porch. For a moment I worried about Jill and her radar, but was soon lost in the spontaneity of the moment. Was this the meaning of spring fever? Abby, never a terrier to miss out, abandoned her chipmunk and galloped over, leaping up and down with us as we danced.

"I have one more gift for you," I told him. "I've ordered my own racing shell from WinTech in Bridgeport. It will be delivered next week, along with oars, and a rack for the dock. It's a two boat deal. Are you interested in keeping your shell here?"

"I'd love it," he said, emphatically. And I knew that he meant more than just the rowing.

"I have a present for you, as well," he said, handing me another small box. "I asked Sophie to hunt this down for me. She ordered it from a place in Edinburgh."

Inside the velvet jeweler's box was a plain gold ring with a flat, round face. A triquetra was engraved in the center.

"I wanted you to have something to remember Hannah. Think of it as a promise ring," he said. "No pressure at all."

Love, Honor, and Protect.

I called Abby and followed Luke inside, very glad that I hadn't bothered to make the bed.

CHAPTER TWENTY-SIX

Felicity

"How's Joy doing, Emma?" Eliot asked. The April Book Club meeting had just concluded. "You've mentioned some difficulties with her training."

I laughed. "All horse show professionals be gone, say I!"

"What now?"

"Oh, the latest is that creepy Frank has Joanne convinced that she is not competent to ride Joy."

"What happened?" Dottie asked. "You always beam when you talk about Joanne!"

"The other day we put up a few cross rails just for fun, so Joanne could see what Joy can do. Joanne was riding. You know how Joy likes to show off. She trotted in to the first jump, and took it at about five and a half feet."

"Wow!" Denise exclaimed.

"It was really cool," I admitted, "except for two things: Joanne nearly got tossed out of the tack from shock, and worse, Frank saw it happen."

"So now he wants to show Joy more than ever," Angela concluded.

"Yep. Ever since then, he's been breaking down Joanne's self esteem, so she'll withdraw from Joy's training, and he'll get my horse. The poor girl is devastated—Frank is rather a name in the jumper world. And of course, it follows that if Joanne is incapable, then I certainly am. Joy's too difficult, she's dangerous, she's inconsistent. Frank insists that I should immediately hand her over to him."

"Regardless of the fact that you have no intention of showing Joy in the jumpers ever again?" Angela asked, angrily.

"Poor Joy!" Dottie sighed. "She never does seem to get a break with these stupid trainers. What are you going to do?"

I grinned, surprising them all. "I'm going to let him show her."

"What?"

"Sure. Joy is smart and super powerful, and she won't tolerate bullies. She'll take care of good ole Frank. Way more effectively than I ever could."

Annie buzzed me at noon. "Gloria from your barn just left a message. She said that Joy is fine, don't worry, but she needs to talk to you."

Gloria picked up in the tack room.

"Emma, have you ever heard of Felicity McDonald?"

"She's the Irish jumper rider who moved here about twenty years ago, won everything, and is now on the U.S. Team."

"Did you know that Frank used to work for her?"

"No. What's going on?"

"He's arranged to have Joy trucked in to Felicity's barn in New Fairfield. He wants to take lessons with Felicity again, and he says that she'll love Joy."

"WITHOUT ASKING HER OWNER FIRST?"

"We all told him that he was way out of line with this. But Meredith overruled us. She said that Frank is Joy's trainer. She said that you should be thrilled to have such a prestigious rider interested in your horse."

"Not to mention the opportunity for Frank!"

"Right."

"When is the trailer leaving?"

"It's already gone, Em. The lesson is scheduled for two o'clock."

Damn.

"I've got a deposition in half an hour. I can't possibly get out of here until after five."

"Joy will probably be back by then."

"I'll be there as soon as I can."

Joy had been turned out in one of the lower paddocks. I opened the gate and she immediately trotted to me. I relaxed a little. She looked sound.

Meredith and her husband Rob came out of the main barn and walked over to us.

"Too bad you missed Frank's lesson, Emma. Felicity was impressed with Joy."

I reminded myself that I had no other barn lined up. Joy would not fit in the back seat of my car.

"Oh really? Did Felicity get on her?"

"For most of the hour. Felicity said that Joy has a lot of talent. Frank is very excited. Felicity has asked him to come back with her next weekend."

"For the whole weekend? Board her there?"

"Yes. I arranged it with Felicity's barn manager."

Rob opened his mouth. "I'll put the trucking charges on your next month's invoice."

Joy and I watched them retreat in the direction of the outdoor ring. She bumped me with her pink and white nose. I produced treats. "Hang in there, honey," I whispered. "This will work out. We'll get Joanne back, and all will be well." She bumped me again, and strode off to look for grass.

Hallie and Lynn met me in the tack room.

"Gloria just told us, Emma. How are you doing?"

"Mostly furious. But I have a feeling that I won't have to put up with this nonsense for long."

"Felicity has a reputation for being hard on the horses. She expects them to be 'stoic.' And she has no patience with free spirited behavior."

"I know."

"Gloria says that Frank is banking on the fact that you aren't going to be able to find another barn around here with a trainer who can handle Joy. He assumes that you have no where else to go."

"That was the one thing keeping me from ripping that smug expression off Meredith's face," I replied. "It was galling. But then again," I smiled, "I know my horse, and they don't. My money's on Joy."

Felicity McDonald was a tall, bleached blond with scrawny legs, no butt, and a round face that had clearly seen too many summers in the sun. She exuded the warmth of Let's Be Friends. I was immediately put on my guard with her.

"Frank, it is yourself!" Felicity beamed at him. "Is the mare ready?"

"Yes. They're bringing her out now. Am I riding, or are you?"

"I'd like a bit of a go on her first," Felicity winked at me. "She's a big girl, isn't she?"

I smiled.

"Do you ride, Emma?"

"I'm learning."

"She'll be a lot of horse for someone who's learning."

"So I've heard."

Frank gave Felicity a leg up and went into the ring with her. I sat on the bench just outside the gate with Gloria. Felicity walked Joy around the ring once in each direction and then picked up a posting trot.

"She uses a lot of arm action, doesn't she?" I asked Gloria.

"Yes, and Joy doesn't seem too thrilled with her methods." We watched them trot over a few poles, Joy's body cranked into a frame: neck arched, head perpendicular with her chest, haunches engaged. Her lower lip was quivering, a sure sign of disfavor. Felicity worked her through some circles and figure eights. Joy began to fuss with her head. Felicity accelerated the jerking action.

"Joy's going to rear," I said.

"Oh yeah," Gloria replied. "There she goes." Joy stood straight up and smashed Felicity's left leg in to the fence rail. Felicity used the crop on her flank. Joy came up again and spun around. Felicity stayed glued to the tack.

"She sure can ride. I'll say that for her," Gloria sighed.

"Set up a five stride!" Felicity yelled to Frank. Joy veered over toward me, and Felicity giggled like a little girl at a coed dance. "She almost had me there," she said. "Come on, Big Mamma, let's jump."

Frank set the distance between the jumps and stood back. Felicity yanked Joy on to the bit again and trotted her to the first fence. Joy cleared the three foot jump easily and cantered to the second. Rather quietly, to my surprise. They repeated this exercise several times. Then Felicity picked up a right lead canter, and she and Joy sailed over every jump in the course.

Finally, they pulled up by us. "That's enough for today, I think," Felicity announced. "Put those poles back, will you Frank love?" She dismounted and called her groom to bring down the next horse. "That went well. The mare will be tired tomorrow. She's got a lot of power, but she needs work."

Gloria and I waited for Frank in the truck. "So much for my

lesson," he growled, as he climbed into the back seat. "I'm going to charge you for my time anyway, Emma. A consulting fee. I got nothing out of today otherwise."

Carlie and I met for dinner at the Tavern.

"So?" She began, with her knack for nosing out information. "Do I detect a new glow about your person? Have you and Luke taken things to the next level?"

A terrier in teenage form.

"Let's just say that I've been getting lots of healthy exercise lately."

Carlie sat back in her chair and finished her ice tea. "Finally! That poor man. I think everyone in town was cheering him on toward the end there. Was it the fancy nightgown from Paris that did the trick?"

I chose to ignore these observations.

"Carlie, I have a proposition for you. As you know, my law partner and I are opening a real satellite office up here. Tina is joining the firm in the Westport office, but I'm overloaded on my own, and I could really use some help. I want to know if you're interested in working for me. It would be part time at first. But the experience will be invaluable if you're still serious about journalism, and it will look great on your college applications."

"Wow Emma," she replied immediately. "That sounds great. I could stay here this summer. What about my parents?" She asked, looking guilty.

"I've already talked to them—they're fine with the idea. They want you to get the most out of your TA education, and you can't do that at home on the farm."

"So I'd live with you? What about Luke?"

"If you can handle it, so can he. Besides, I can always go to his place, and you can have Julie over. Or you can spend the night at her house."

Carlie was processing a whole new concept of summer vacation. "One other thing honey. Your sixteenth birthday is coming up—May is just around the corner. Your parents and I have decided to split the price of a car for you."

"Woo-hoo!" Carlie shrieked.

"I've found a previously owned VW Beetle convertible. It's light green—in great shape—fun to drive. Your parents are covering the insurance, and they're mailing the plates down here." I pulled a copy of the CT driver's manual out of my purse. "Start studying!"

The Connecticut Alliance of Professional Women had agreed to present a program to the students of Tallmadge Academy for Girls on the subject of empowerment for young women. The entire school, including most of the staff, had foregathered in the auditorium. The new Headmistress, Dr. Barnes, introduced Denise and myself as Co-Chairs. Then Denise took the podium.

"We are an affiliation of professional women," she said, "committed to supporting individuals during major life transitions such as family challenges, divorce, retirement, widowhood, and career changes." Denise smiled. "Becoming an adult is a pretty big transition as well, and we're here to help. Our mission is to provide a holistic approach that will dispel myths, alleviate fears, and empower the public through education.

"We have members who are licensed CPAs," she continued, "financial planners and advisors, and mortgage and insurance specialists. We also have career advisors, mental health professionals, and attorneys who work with civil and family matters, as well as trusts and estates, and elder law."

Denise introduced Liz Klein, who spoke to the group about effective methods of assembling a resume, and narrowing the focus with career choices. "I understand that most, if not all of you, are college bound, and beyond. I encourage every student in this room to go back to your dorm tonight, and make a list of the subjects that you enjoy studying, and the kind of work that you prefer doing. You'll be amazed how helpful it is to see these items in print. For example—are you an independent person, or are you more productive in groups? Are you a leader, or a teacher, or do you require more structure in your life? Are you drawn to certain issues? Think about it."

Carol Porto from Warwick Mortgage discussed the importance of a good credit rating, and issued a strong warning about banks and interest rates. "Unfortunately we are living in a culture that is based on credit, which in my opinion, is destroying the economy. My advice to all of you is to start a trend back toward the old cash on the barrel philosophy. Avoid credit cards. The interest rates are staggering, and the only people who gain from them are the banks. You can easily maintain a good credit rating by paying your utilities on time. Keep a gas card if you must, but pay it off every month. If you decide that you want to buy a home and you need a mortgage, shop around carefully. Be aware that some companies will only offer you their product. You have options. Finally, keep copies of your rent checks for at least a year, and make sure that you always pay all your bills on time."

Jean Corbett talked about health insurance, and reiterated Carol's advice regarding the importance of shopping carefully before signing. "Read your policy thoroughly," she stressed. "Make sure you know exactly what your coverage is, what your deductible is, and what pitfalls, if any, are attached. Your doctors may or may not work with your carrier. Know this before you commit."

Nan Richardson, a trusts and estates attorney, spoke regarding the importance of estate planning. "Whether or not you are married and have children," she said, "and especially if you are commingling funds with someone, make sure that your interests and rights are protected. Get it all in writing as soon as possible."

Tracy O'Brien, the group CPA, discussed the importance of good tax advice. "The government is always looking for a way to squeeze more money out of you," she warned. "Make sure you know what you're getting into. For example—many people don't realize that if they take money out of an IRA before they reach retirement age, the government gets a huge cut—and then you *still* have to pay taxes on it. Do extensive research, and by all means, get professional advice before you do anything with your money."

Denise got up to address the realities of divorce. "I'm sure you're thinking that high school students are much too young to be hearing about the topics that we've been discussing today. And you'd be incorrect. Our aim is to teach you to be empowered now—so that you don't make the common mistakes that Attorney Carbury and I see in our offices—every day. Women have been acculturated to fear money. This is the reason that so many talented, educated women suddenly find themselves in crisis situations with a failed marriage, and no access to funds. Maintain your financial independence, no matter what. You want to avoid having some elderly man in a robe—socially and legally stuck somewhere around 1955—deciding your financial future."

Our final speaker was Miranda Pollack, Ph.D. "Have we scared you yet?" Randy asked.

Everyone laughed.

"OK. Once again, the key to self empowerment is education. Nothing breeds fear and indecision faster than ignorance. And as we know from our studies of world history, bad things happen when people insist on remaining in the dark.

"Having said that, let's talk for a bit about bullying."

Denise and I met Luke for dinner at the Tavern after the CAPW program had concluded.

"It went very well, Luke," I told him. "Denise and the other women woke those girls up with a bang."

"Yes," Denise agreed. "Hopefully tonight they're thinking about something other than designer shoes and getting the right boyfriend."

"We have to keep it up," I reminded her. "The Headmistress is on board. We're going to give the students regular injections of reality from now on."

"Have you talked to the BHS Headmaster?" Luke asked. "Because it sounds as though this information would benefit the boys as well."

"Dr. Barnes said that she'd arrange a meeting with him this week," Denise announced. "She also gave Emma a huge compliment. Barnes called you TA's Warrior, Em. She said that you and your spies have changed the climate of the school forever, and saved it from a probable media disaster. The Headmistress said that the Board, the staff, and every student and alum owe you a huge debt of gratitude."

"Wow," I said shakily, extremely embarrassed. "Maybe they'll give me a pay raise next year."

I walked Denise to her car after dinner. "Lovely man, Emma. Well done! No wonder you want to spend more time up here."

I looked over at Luke, who was standing by our cars. "He's pretty special, I agree."

"Well, make sure you let him know that. A lot," she said, hugging me. "Under all that manly physique, Luke's a pretty sensitive person. You need to feed him, as much as he's feeding you. And he is, I can feel it. He's serious."

"I know how lucky I am! Don't worry. I want this to work."

"Good. Just remember—he's lucky too."

CHAPTER TWENTY-SEVEN

Joy and Frank

Abby and I arrived at the Turner Farm Horse Show at eight in the morning. Apple Ridge had rented temporary stalls that were set up in one of the tents on the hill beyond the indoor. I located the apple green and yellow show drapes. There were several show tack trunks lined up in the main aisle. I scanned for my monogram. My trunk was not in evidence.

Rory, the assistant barn manager, was in the feed stall. "Where's my trunk, Rory?"

"We didn't bring it. You're not showing."

"But my horse is. Where is Joy's tack?"

"It's in a couple of the farm trunks. They're pretty heavy to transport, you know."

"Did I pay less for the commercial trucker to move Joy over here than everyone else did?"

"Well, no."

"Was this your decision, or Frank's?"

"Mine."

"I want my trunk in this tent by tomorrow morning, is that clear? I will not have my expensive equipment floating all over these show grounds."

Rory's eyes hardened. "Fine." I watched her pull out her cell phone and move to the other end of the aisle.

I found Carlos brushing Joy in one of the grooming stalls.

"Do you know when Joy's trip is going to be, Carlos?"

"I think she's third. She was very good yesterday. You should have seen her."

"I heard that she won the schooling jumper class. That's great. Do you know where Frank is?"

"Buying coffee, he said."

"I'll get some breakfast then. Would you like anything?"

"An egg sandwich, *por favor*." He fished in his pocket for cash.

"I've got it. Anything to drink?"

"Just water. *Gracias*."

Abby and I walked over to the food tent. Frank, who was sitting at one of the tables with a group of women that I didn't know, completely ignored me. I ordered two egg and cheese on hard rolls. Behind me, the rings were filling up with people and horses. The young hunters, with their manes and tails beautifully braided, were schooling with their trainers. The grand prix field was set for the low preliminary jumper class, with jumps of four feet to four three, and oxer spreads of four to four foot six. Joy loved to gallop in grass, as long as it was dry.

My number was called to pick up the sandwiches. Frank had disappeared. I saw him in the field a moment later, walking the course with his clack of female jumper professionals. Abby and I headed back to the tent. Joy was tacked up and stood quietly on the cross ties, covered with her new show cooler. She looked beautiful. Her dark brown hair gleamed with red highlights, and her pink and white muzzle was spotless. Her feet, black in front and white in back, shone with hoof polish. I checked to make sure that Carlos had remembered to screw the caulks into her shoes for the grass field. Then I patted her neck and she bumped my pockets, sniffing for treats. I produced a mint, which she accepted delicately.

Frank appeared at the doorway of the tent. "If you're done with your breakfast, Carlos," he snarled, "we can get down to the schooling ring." Carlos finished his egg sandwich in two bites, took a swig of water, and led Joy out to the driveway. He gave Frank a leg up and then grabbed his grooming box, following them down the hill. Abby and I stayed a safe distance behind.

Gloria caught up to us. "Sorry about the trunk snafu, Em," She apologized. "Rory was covering for Frank."

"Let me guess," I replied. "He's got a leg over her as well as Meredith?"

Gloria grinned. "That's the talk at the water cooler. No confirmation though. By the way, did you notice Joy's bit?"

"Yes, why? That's the Pelham that she always shows in."

"He tried her in a gag bit yesterday."

"Why the hell did he do that? He should have checked with me. Joy hates gag bits."

"That became apparent very quickly. She dumped him in front of everyone in the jumper schooling area. Then he put her in the Pelham with a figure eight nose band."

I was speechless with rage.

"Joy responded by spinning around and smashing him into a jump standard. He stayed on that time, though."

"That jerk! I TOLD him exactly what tack she shows in, and why. There's a reason why I have her in a plain hunter nose band."

"Joy got her way in the end," Gloria chuckled. "She always does."

"And she still won the class. What a trooper she is! Well, that explains the hostility this morning."

The gate keeper called the line up. "Karla is in the ring, with

Elinor on deck, then Frank, John, and Roberta. Let's keep it moving people. There are forty horses in this class."

We watched Carlos scurrying around, setting jumps in the warm up ring, which per usual, was a picture of utter chaos. Huge horses, mostly European warmbloods, ridden by professionals, careened from every corner. Trainers shouted at grooms, while over head the loudspeaker boomed at regular intervals. "Elinor is in the ring. Frank, you're on deck. Then John, Roberta, Patrick, Shirley and Hope. Keep them coming, folks."

Abby was nose to nose with two Jack Russell males. I held my breath, but the dogs all wagged their tails in a friendly fashion. Abby could be quite the flirt when she chose.

Carlos brushed Joy's legs, and wiped Frank's boots. Elinor and her big gray gelding knocked down two rails, totaling eight faults. They walked out of the ring as Frank and Joy walked in.

"This is number three forty nine, Ballygowan Joy, owned by Emma Carbury of Bridge Hollow, Connecticut. Frank Shaw is her rider."

The buzzer sounded and they began the course. Joy was in her element. Frank tried to hold her back for the first few fences, but finally gave up. Joy was all business about her job, and she could turn her long powerful body with amazing agility and speed. They were clean in the first round, well under the time limit, and then clean in the jump off.

"That moves Ballygowan Joy into first place," Announcer Man informed us.

Gloria looked around. "No sign of Felicity. Maybe she's not coming until this weekend. I know she's riding in the Grand Prix on Sunday."

It would be a while before the class was over, and we heard the results, but it was definitely a good start to the day. Back at the tent I gave Joy an apple and some carrots, kissed her nose, and thanked

Carlos. I noticed that Joy's blue ribbon from her schooling jumper class was hung on the farm banner over the tent entrance. I managed to get Abby back into the car and drive out without ever exchanging one word with Frank. The man had the manners of a gorilla.

The following week I dropped by the barn early before work to say hello to Joy. Gloria was doing feed in the main aisle.

"You're really brave to come in here in that suit."

"Where's Rory lately? I thought she did the morning feed."

"Didn't you hear? She's pregnant. She went back to Middleburg to have the baby."

"Is she saying who the father is?"

Gloria dropped Jasper's grain in his bucket and turned to stare at me.

"NO!"

"Of course, Emma. Why do you think she was always covering for him? When Meredith became interested, it wasn't long until Rory was out the door."

"But Weasel Frank? Rory's such a nice girl!"

"And he's such a big name in the jumper world. The show circuit isn't exactly over run with men who like women. At least not in this country. So I'm sure that the temptation was high."

"And the gene pool low. I wondered why there was such a change in her personality. She seemed to shrivel up overnight."

"That must have been about the time that Frank blew her off. It was brutal, but effective. He got her to leave the Tri-State area. Maybe for good."

"And I took her behavior toward Joy so personally!"

"At least you have the satisfaction of knowing that Rory's attitude had nothing to do with you, or your horse."

"What's the schedule for this weekend?"

"Last I heard, Joy is being trucked over to Felicity's on Friday afternoon. She'll spend the weekend working with Felicity and Frank, getting her ready for the Clover Brook Farm show in New York. She's doing both weeks there, right?"

"As far as I know. He's starting her in schooling jumpers first, to warm her up in the field before the prelims."

"Have you got an extra set of caulks for her shoes?"

"In my trunk. I hope it doesn't rain. Joy won't jump if the grass is too wet."

"I'll tell Frank." Gloria dumped the last grain bucket and started rolling the cart back to the feed room. "Come to Fox Ledge on Saturday. A bunch of us are going to watch Felicity torture Frank. Should be a good time."

"It would be a much better time if he was riding someone else's horse."

The following week Gloria called me at the Westport office. "Frank has decided to show Joy in the high preliminary jumpers— instead of the low class."

I was in the middle of drafting a difficult mediation agreement. "What? Why?"

"Felicity wants him to. She made an unexpected appearance this morning and had him scratch Joy's entry in the lows. The high prelim class just finished."

"How'd she do?"

"Fifth. She got a rail in the jump off, but it really wasn't her fault. It was a tough course, and Frank was hanging on her mouth and crawling up her neck, as usual."

"I appreciate your calling Gloria. I won't be able to make it to the show until Friday morning."

"You're welcome. Joy's a terrific mare. She just needs respectful handling, and Frank is not that kind of rider."

"No. He most definitely is not."

Joy's high preliminary jumper class on Friday was to be held in the grand prix field. I had arranged to meet Gloria and Hallie in the stands when the class began. It had rained heavily the night before, and I was concerned about the footing. Several trainers had already decided to scratch their entries.

"Frank's still planning to ride, Emma," Gloria said as she handed me an ice tea.

"Thanks."

"He says that fewer horses means a better chance at a good ribbon."

"He's still ticked off about yesterday, I gather?"

"He's furious that he didn't get a prize, and he's blaming Joy. Says that she wasn't focused at all."

"That tells me that she's so tired, she's not even trying."

"At this height, that can be dangerous."

"I know."

We watched two trips go around the course. Both horses appeared to have difficulty making the turns in the wet grass. The third horse nearly slid into the last jump. I could feel the stomach acid rising in my throat.

"I'm going to stop this," I said to Gloria.

Frank was warming up in the schooling area. Joy's legs were plastered with sand, and her eyes, normally relaxed and friendly, were wide open and staring. I walked to the rail and called to Frank.

"I'm pulling her out of this class. The field is too sloppy."

"WHAT!"

"You heard me. I don't want Joy to get hurt. She's had enough. She's done here."

Frank jumped down to the ground and threw the reins to Carlos. He ran over to me, waving his crop around his head.

"I'M the trainer here! YOU don't make the decisions! I DO!"

That's when it happened.

Joy sounded her battle roar. Everyone in the ring watched in horror as she tore away from Carlos and galloped straight for Frank. He turned, just as more than twelve hundred pounds of enraged Irish Sport mare stood up in front of him. I saw one black hoof flash, and Frank was airborne.

Connecticut General Statutes section 52-557p states in pertinent part: "Each person engaged in recreational equestrian activities shall assume the risk and legal responsibility for any injury to his person or property arising out of the hazards inherent in equestrian sports[.]"

I considered the question of whether the law applied similarly to equestrian professionals when injured over the state line in New York, just as Frank landed in a heap by a trash can.

Gloria called after dinner that night. "Three broken ribs and a dislocated shoulder. He's lucky. It could have been much worse. Either way, he's out of riding commission for the rest of the season."

"He can still teach, though." I sighed. "I guess I'm supposed to feel some sympathy. Not to say guilt."

"Do you?"

"Nope. Not a smidge of either."

"Well, why should you? From where I sat, if Frank hadn't ended up in the hospital, it might have been you. There were plenty of witnesses."

"I got some of their names, just in case."

"I heard about the scene with Felicity."

"Oh yes. That was delightful."

"What did she say? I was too busy with the ambulance guys."

"She made a big point of reminding me about her 'level' of riding as she announced that if *she* had difficulty with Joy, then I *certainly* couldn't handle her."

"Has she ever seen you ride?"

"She was completely undeterred by the fact that she doesn't know a blessed thing about me, or the relationship that Joy and I have. The best part was when she summarily determined to get Joy ready for sale."

"What did you say to that?"

"I couldn't beat her to death with my purse, tempting as that was, so I just walked away. I figured no one would buy the story that I was attacked by two crazed horse professionals in the space of a few minutes."

"Understandable reaction. Felicity is all about ego. The good news is that Joy seems OK. I just checked on her."

"I had a long talk with her before I left the show," I admitted. "Mostly it involved groveling. I apologized over and over for putting her through this torture. I said that from now on, her safety and happiness are my priorities, barn location be damned. I informed her that I would get Joanne back working with us immediately. Finally, I promised her fresh produce every day."

"How did she react to this embarrassing display of humility?"

"She bumped me with her nose, and then offered her butt for scratching."

"That means she's still good with you," Gloria laughed.

"Must be. Joy's too smart to ever turn her back on an enemy."

Hallie met me for lunch at the Warren Inn. We were seated on the terrace, with a marvelous view of the lake. The waiter brought us large ice teas and Caesar salads with grilled shrimp.

"You are obviously bursting with information!" I laughed. "Please feel free to relieve the strain."

Hallie leaned forward, gleeful. "Rob caught them in the act! He hired a private investigator and nailed Meredith and Frank, er, nailing each other!"

"Eureka! Rob finally grew a set!"

"The best part is that a couple who live in Manhattan have offered to buy the farm, and Meredith has decided to accept. The new owners will only be around on weekends and holidays, so Gloria is staying on as manager, and Frank is out! They're bringing in a woman from Massachusetts to take over the hunter/jumper clients, and Joanne will continue to teach dressage."

I was amazed. "We got everything we wanted Hallie! We're keeping the great facility and the wonderful people, but the horrors are going."

Another example of Universal stage managing.

Hallie raised her glass. "Life is good! The new people ride dressage, so they're putting in a dressage ring next month. The paddocks near the indoor will be replaced by our own lovely arena. No jumping, no lunging, no kids on ponies. Now we can concentrate on our flat work, really dance, without dodging twenty-seven jumps and fifty-eight poles in the outdoor."

"Hopefully this new jumping trainer knows her stuff, so Joy and I can occasionally do fun, little courses. No more showing, no more gigantic oxers." I grinned as I buttered my roll. "I promised Joy. And one never goes back on one's word to Joy."

"Not if one wants to live!" Hallie replied.

CHAPTER TWENTY-EIGHT

Founder's Day Ball

"Hello Gorgeous!" Luke exclaimed. "Amazing dress!" I twirled as best as I could, given the yards of material that extended behind me.

"I had it made in town," I explained, picking up my wrap, and my evening bag.

"What do you call that color blue? It's unusual, isn't it?"

"It was the color of Hannah's riding habit—so I wanted to match it. Midnight blue? I'm not sure." I had had my hair put in a twist, with a sparkly comb on one side.

Luke was still staring at me.

"Too much like the portrait?" I asked him.

He smiled and offered me his arm. "No. I was just thinking how incredibly happy I am."

"Nice tuxedo by the way," I said after a few minutes, smudging the lipstick on his mouth with my fingers. "Very James Bond."

Morse Mansion was located at the north end of Main Street, right on the Hunterbury River. Built in 1750, it had been part of a large estate at one time, but was now owned by the town of Bridge Hollow, and rented out for events. The three story white house was surrounded by a wide porch, now teeming with guests for the Ball. Luke dropped me off on the circular driveway, and drove on to the parking area. I gathered my gown with one hand and proceeded up the stairs. Enormous floral arrangements flanked the double doors, and white lights were twinkling everywhere. I presented my ticket, and was offered a glass of champagne from a passing server.

About half of the assembly had come in costume. There were powdered wigs, period dresses, colonial officers and soldiers, and even a few redcoats.

I saw Sophie and waved. She was standing in one corner of the big entry hall with the Tallmadge Academy psychiatrist, Karl Skinner. Sophie beckoned me over.

"Emma, you look lovely! I think you know Karl," she said. Karl and I greeted each other.

"It's a pleasure, Attorney Carbury. The Board is quite impressed by you, and by the efforts of your students. You have many fans."

"Thank you, Dr. Skinner," I said, equally politely.

"I am especially grateful on Julia's behalf," he continued.

"Julia?" I asked, confused.

"I probably should have mentioned this before, Emma," Sophie said, apologetically. "Karl is Julie's father."

At that moment another server came by, bless the man. I exchanged my empty champagne flute for a fresh one.

"There you are!" Luke said, from behind me. "Good evening Sophie. Karl."

Saved again.

"Do you mind if I drag Emma off to the buffet?" Luke asked.

"Not at all," Sophie replied, clearly amused.

"Luke!" I whispered, when we had progressed a safe distance. "I thought Skinner was supposed to be gay!"

"He is. That's his partner over there." He indicated a tall man, at least ten years Karl's junior.

"Oh!" I paused to pick up a plate. "Did you know that he was Julie's dad?"

"That's been the rumor for years," Luke replied, absorbed in the selection of meats.

"Poor Julie! Her mother's a witch and her father prefers men. Even in this enlightened twenty-first century, that's a lot for a kid to swallow."

"It certainly explains Julie's reserved personality. Hats off to Carlie, for getting through to her."

"Speak of the future journalist, here she is."

Carlie and some of the girls from her floor had decided to dress as members of the Connecticut militia for the occasion. Her dark blond hair was pulled back in a pony tail and tied with a navy ribbon. On her head was a tri cornered hat.

"Great get up!" Luke exclaimed. "I wouldn't have recognized you."

"I'll hold your musket honey, so you can get some food." I said.

"Thanks! This thing's heavy." Carlie picked up a plate. "Hey Emma, isn't that your office share female? The one who was so tight with Yolanda Gibbs?"

I turned to look. "That's Valerie. She and her husband slash law partner are splitting up, so I got out of that office just in time. I don't know what happened."

"I do," Carlie grinned. "They were talking about it at the boathouse. Apparently Tom was sleeping with the receptionist."

"This town is way too small," I commented.

Carlie had no sympathy. "Small!" She snorted. "You should see where I live! At least here, the humans outnumber the cows. I'm going to find Julie."

Lexie stopped us on our way to sit down.

"Fabulous party, Alexandra! I hope you're pleased."

"They all seem to be having a good time," she agreed, looking around. "We had a big turn out from the other boarding schools. Everyone's making new friends."

"I see that." Hormones were bouncing off the walls inside the mansion. It was beginning to affect me.

"I wanted to thank you one more time, Ms. Carbury—without you—I wouldn't have known what to do."

"It was a team effort, Lexie. You've got a lot of courage. It was your testimony that really swayed the Board. Remember that."

She smiled and moved off.

Luke and I had located seats when Prue, the rowing therapist turned hockey player, approached us, and took a seat next to Luke. She greeted us both.

"How are things with the She Lions, Prue?" I asked. "I hear that you and the ladies did well this year."

"We did," Prue beamed, "and I want to thank you again for helping me that day in the locker room. I'm happier doing what I want to do, which makes my husband and the kids happier."

Luke glanced at me. Was he worried that I'd grow wings and a halo and fly off?

"Glad to hear it. Are you enjoying Founder's Weekend?"

She finished her champagne. "Very much. Especially all the costumes. Well, I'll leave you both to your dinners."

"Emma?"

"Yes Luke?"

"Why do I feel as though I'm one of the bit players in *It's a Wonderful Life*, and you're in the starring role?"

I put my plate down and proceeded to break my rule against public display of affection. For several minutes.

"Feel better?"

He nodded. "It's nice here in the bit parts."

"My dear man," I replied. "There is nothing 'bit part' about you."

The band started up in the ballroom, and everyone slowly made their way inside.

"We've only danced together once before," Luke whispered.

"We dance all the time," I whispered back. "This time we'll be doing it upright."

Abby was waiting impatiently by the door when we got back to my house. Luke said he'd get the fireplace going upstairs, while I changed my heels for garden clogs, and went out to the back yard with her.

"Have some mercy, Abs," I said, as she galloped off in front of me. "Don't take too long."

I walked out on to the dock, and stood staring at the water, marveling at the beautiful reflections of the moon and stars on the surface. The moon, almost full, was just rising above the tree line.

I heard footsteps behind me. A colonial soldier was standing at the edge of the dock.

"Carlie? I thought you were staying in the dorm tonight."

The soldier suddenly ran forward, and in a second I realized that this person was too big to be Carlie.

He swung the butt of his musket straight at my head. Clumsy in my gown and clogs, I barely had time to dodge him. He moved in closer. Then, from somewhere near my feet, I heard the rumbling of a terrier incensed. The man howled with pain, dropped the musket, and kicked out.

There came a sound from my little dog so ferocious, I froze where I stood. Abby launched herself at the soldier, and sank her teeth into his knee.

At that moment, I found my lawyer voice, and yelled as I hadn't done since I was married to my first husband.

Suddenly Luke was there. The moon came out as he grabbed

the man, and we both stared in shock. The colonial soldier was Therese Ellis.

And then, sirens. I would never again complain about snoopy neighbors. Jill had taken the hint, for once in her life, and called the police.

"Are you liking the script better Luke?" I asked, once our statements had been taken, and Therese had been driven away.

"What a busy life you do lead, Emma!" He said, rubbing his arm. "That was one strong, crazy young woman. You and Abby had the situation under control between you, but I'm glad that I was here to help."

Love, Honor, and Protect.

I looked at him, still in his tuxedo, and felt the thrill of the moon's energy. I moved closer and ran my hand slowly down his back.

CHAPTER TWENTY-NINE

Healing Spell

Sophie had us assemble along the Woodruff foot bridge between the two schools.

"What's the weight limit on this thing?" Carlie asked me.

"Shhh!"

"As this place marks the link between Bridge Hollow School for
Boys," Sophie began, "and the drowning of a student that occurred
there in early 1780—and Tallmadge Academy for Girls, and its
tragedy of 1952, I feel this bridge is the proper spot energetically
to cast our spell."

A group of students, female and male, had lined up on the
bridge, and on both banks of the river, to take part in the working of this magick. The new TA Headmistress, Dr. Martha Barnes,
stood at one end of the bridge, and the BHS Headmaster, Charles
Bakewell, at the other. Luke had gathered men and women from
Masters rowing on the BHS dock.

Emma's Spies clustered around Sophie, myself, and Carlie,
Lexie, and Julie. Every person was holding a burning candle. Fires
had been lit in several portable pits, creating blazing light on both
sides of the bridge. The river sparkled with reflections from the
flames.

It was twilight on June twentieth—the eve of the Summer Solstice.

"This time is known as Midsummer," Sophie began, her voice echoing over the water. "The longest day of the year. It is a Sabbat from the ancient Celtic calendar, and its festival honors life, and the bounty of the natural world. The Summer Solstice is the perfect holiday to work Fire magick—bringing in Fire energy. Fire represents the Sun at the zenith of its power. It is a masculine energy. It is connected with transformation, and with courage. Its color is red, and its direction is South. Therefore, you all will face the lake as we work this spell.

"We are asking for Transformation for both of these schools. For everyone who has gone before—especially for Christopher Marsh and Anna Crawford—and for every student from now on. We will be performing healing magick tonight.

"I have asked you all to write on small pieces of paper something in your lives that you want to be done with. Some aspect of yourself that you wish to banish.

"First you will ground yourselves. Stamp your feet, and imagine roots dropping down from your body, anchoring you to the earth. Visualize a white light of protection surrounding all of us. I will summon the four Directions, and the Elements, with a special emphasis on Fire. I will then invite a healing transformation. Once this is done, I will ask you to raise the energy level of this assembly. Please do whatever makes you comfortable—you may dance, or spin in place, or run, or wave your arms—or stand and stamp."

Sophie paused. "Imagine that you are at a pep rally, before a big game, and raising energy will become easier."

There was laughter.

"When the time is right, I will ask you to put your paper into the fire. As you do this, please send your passion regarding your request into the flames. The fire will consume and purify it. I will then ask you to ground yourselves again, and we will be done."

The energy raised from our combined efforts was so intense that we all could feel it, as though the heat from the flames was enclosing, and changing us. Waves and waves of positive emotion billowed as the students began dancing around the fire pits, and the rowers on the dock executed jumping jacks—creating waves that splashed against the bank of the river. Dr. Barnes was power walking on an invisible treadmill. Carlie and I, hampered by lack of space, danced the Twist. Lexie and Julie grabbed hands and twirled. Heather and Jeanne waltzed in place. The little bridge bounced from the strain. Carlie glanced at me, registering dismay.

And suddenly, Sophie lifted her arms. I knew that she was visualizing the Cone of Power. She took Julie's candle, and lit the two lanterns in front of her on the bridge, releasing our healing magick to the Universe.

"One if by land, two if by sea," Carlie murmured.

"I think the lanterns represent Christopher and Anna," I whispered back.

Carlie heaved a big sigh. "Honestly Emma," she said.

"Everyone please send your requests to the fire," Sophie shouted. "And then ground your energy once more."

I moved across the bridge to the BHS side and located Luke, who had just tossed his paper into the flames. I did the same, and put my arm around him. We stepped back to watch the others.

"Do you mind if I ask?" Luke said to me, quietly.

"Not at all," I replied, circling his waist with my other arm. "My request was to banish 'fear of intimacy' from my life." He hugged me in return. "What was yours?" I asked.

"The same," Luke whispered.

Carlie and I had a rowing date before she went home to Vermont to spend a few weeks with her family.

I was using my new Wintech lightweight racing shell, which I loved. I had ordered my full name done in a decal for both sides of the bow, and took tremendous satisfaction in knowing that I was now free from group rowing forevermore.

Carlie, having borrowed Luke's much longer boat, was having some trouble steering.

"That's what you get for sticking to sweep," I chortled. "You need to mix it up now and then, or you'll forget what to do with your other hand."

"Ha ha." Carlie replied. She managed to back her shell into position, and we took off at a leisurely stroke away from the river.

"So? What did you think of your first year at Tallmadge Academy?" I asked her.

"Uh, a little more action than I had originally bargained for," she grimaced, "but a good time overall. I'm loving the whole reporter thing. I've received rave reviews from the administration for my coverage on Founder's Day weekend, and especially for the joint school healing spell. We got some great shots of all the fires and candles—before it got too dark. It was a real special interest piece. Please thank Luke again when you see him."

"For allowing you to tell Hannah and Zachary's story? Of course. I think he knew that it was time that the truth was released. I had all those dreams for a reason! Perhaps Hannah, in her way, was encouraging me to speak up on her behalf."

"On everyone's behalf, really. Look at what your Evidence class started Emma! If Lexie hadn't felt that she could trust you, maybe nothing at all would have been accomplished. Who knows where she'd be right now! Probably in some mental ward, on a whole bunch of pills that would never help her. And whacko Therese would have been crowned Queen of Founder's Weekend, or something just as nauseating. Face it Emma—I may have been your chief spy, but you were definitely the leader in charge."

"I feel like I've been channeling the General all year!" I joked. "Now, if I could only ride the way he did!"

"You're cooped up in rings too much," Carlie said. "That's your problem. Boundaries may be great in relationships, but in my opinion, horses weren't made to go round and round inside a fence. I think you should take Luke up on his offer, and ship Joy up there regularly. He and I both grew up riding on big farms. If you fell off—oh well. In Washington's day, horses were all they had for transportation. Those people had to be great in the saddle."

"And the women!" I exclaimed. "In long skirts, with only one leg on the horse. I was galloping about in my dreams as Hannah— that woman could certainly handle her mare!"

"No comment on the stupidity of the sidesaddle," Carlie said, drily. "As far as I'm concerned, they were just another way that men kept women disempowered. But your dreams may have had a whole other meaning besides past life stuff."

"Get on my horse and ride?"

"Precisely. Forget the competitive nonsense. Blow off the show barn scene. It's all BS anyway."

We rowed on in silence for a bit.

"Do you think you'll marry Luke?" Carlie asked, suddenly. "Because I definitely get the feeling that's what he wants."

"Really? Why?"

"The ring, for one thing. Guys don't give out friendship rings anymore, Emma. He's serious."

"I'm serious too. But that doesn't necessarily presume that marriage is the next step."

"How come?"

"Because women no longer need men to support them. Historically, marriage was about the joining of property between two families. Money, and keeping the family line going. It was never about romance or love. It *can* be, I grant you. But freedom is a wonderful thing, Carlie. Especially when you've lost it for a time, and you remember what it feels like to be trapped and miserable in an unhappy relationship."

"But Luke would never treat you like Joshua treated Hannah."

"Of course he wouldn't. But that's not the point. Sometimes people just change. They find new interests. They're lazy, or bored, and they stop trying. Abuse isn't the only reason to end a marriage! And divorce is a god awful process. Strangers butting into your personal business. The state is suddenly sleeping in your bedroom, raising your kids, and balancing your checkbook."

Carlie called weigh enough. We stopped, our oars feathered above the water.

"OK," she said, turning to me, "then why do people bother?"

"Social conditioning? Religion? Family pressures? Government promising lower taxes? I honestly don't know."

"I think that marriage is about commingling souls."

"What? Where on earth did you hear that?"

Carlie looked sheepish. "A movie. It sounded so nice though. You know, two people sharing their lives like that."

"It does sound great. But why do you need to get married? Luke and I are doing that now, with two separate homes, and two very different careers."

"What if a couple wants kids?"

"Lots of people who aren't married have kids these days, honey. Many women are going to sperm banks so they can avoid male partners altogether."

"Then I'm confused," she replied, suddenly childish. "And a little upset. My parents are happy."

"I'm sure they are. But they're lucky—trust me."

"So you're saying basically—what? Act married, just don't make it official, so you don't have to get divorced?"

"Partly," I said, wanting to be careful. "Act married, with a serious written contract in place if you need to—so everyone's rights are protected."

"Are you and Luke going to do that?"

"Not right now, no. We don't need to. Our financial positions are totally independent. But say in a few years he decides to plant a vineyard, or sell organic produce, or I don't know—buy a herd of milking goats and make cheese. And I decide to invest in that with him. If we were just colleagues doing a business deal, there'd be a contract, right? But for some reason, once people start having sex, their business sense goes out the window, and they don't protect themselves. Years of valuable time and effort are lost."

Carlie pondered this. "I think I'm seeing daylight. You're saying that women should look out for themselves financially, even if they're in a relationship."

"Women *and* men. Unfortunately, it's nearly always the women who lose. Men tend to be much more sensible about the bottom line."

"Women like Hannah—you mean?"

"Yes. Today we are earning advanced degrees and professional licenses, and yet so many of us still seem stuck in Hannah's time period."

"Lexie and I talked about that," Carlie remarked, as we resumed rowing. "About women wasting their brains. Did you hear that she got accepted to Vanderbilt? But she's decided to go to Washington University in St. Louis instead. She wants to be closer to home."

"I don't blame her."

"Lexie has decided to be a lawyer, like you," Carlie continued. "She wants to help women and children."

"I applaud her community spirit. However, I've learned that teaching young people to avoid mistakes is a hell of a lot more satisfying than getting them out of the soup later on."

"That's why I'm going to be a journalist," Carlie replied. "If I expose the jerks, women and children will be safer."

"Then consider freelance work, honey. Remember, if you're reporting to people who are signing your paycheck, their opinion—and who's paying *them*—will sway what they want you to write."

"I know," Carlie said, a little glum. "But I have to start somewhere. And I need to be thinking about where I want to go to school, so I can gear my activities for the next two years in that direction."

"Why don't you cast a spell to help you decide what to do?"

Carlie giggled. "That's a good idea! Something like

I'm in a dilemma,
Talked it over with Emma.
What major do I choose,
Help me Universe and send a Muse."

I laughed. "And how about a big finish? Sort of borrowed from the Beatles?

I want to start a Revolution,
Let's bring this Earth some Evolution!"

"I like it!" Carlie grinned. "So Mote It Be!"

It does not require a majority to prevail, but rather an irate,
tireless minority keen to set brush fires in people's minds.

SAMUEL ADAMS
AUGUST 1, 1776

RECOMMENDED READING

Washington's Spies, The Story of America's First Spy Ring by Alexander Rose, Bantam Dell (2006).

Setting the World Ablaze, Washington, Adams, Jefferson, and the American Revolution by John Ferling, Oxford University Press (2000).

The Ascent of George Washington, The Hidden Political Genius of an American Icon by John Ferling, Bloomsbury Press (2009).

Washington, A Life by Ron Chernow, The Penguin Press (2010).

My Dearest Friend, Letters of Abigail and John Adams Edited by Margaret A. Hogan and C. James Taylor, The Belknap Press of Harvard University Press (2007).

Abigail & John, Portrait of a Marriage by Edith B. Gelles, Harper Perennial (2009).

Liberty! The American Revolution by Thomas Fleming, Viking Penguin (1997).

The History of the Town of Litchfield, Connecticut 1720-1920 by Alain C. White, Higginson Book Company (1920).

Unfinished Business, What the Dead Can Teach Us About Life by James Van Praagh, HarperCollins (2009).

Past Lives, Future Healing by Sylvia Browne with Lindsay Harrison, New American Library (2001).

Voices from the Other Side of the Couch: A Warrior's View of Shamanic Healing by John Myerson & Judith Robbins, Life Arts Press (2008).

Queen Bees & Wannabes by Rosalind Wiseman, Three Rivers Press (2002, 2009).

Queen Bee Moms & King Pin Dads by Rosalind Wiseman with Elizabeth Rapoport, Three Rivers Press (2006).

The Bully, the Bullied, and the Bystander by Barbara Coloroso, HarperCollins (2003).

Girl Wars by Cheryl Dellasega, Ph.D., and Charisse Nixon, Ph.D., Fireside (2003).

The Complete Guide to Understanding, Controlling, and Stopping Bullies & Bullying by Margaret R. Kohut, MSW, Atlantic Publishing Group, Inc. (2007).

The Bully Action Guide by Edward F. Dragan, EdD, Palgrave MacMillan (2011).

Bully Police . . . . www.bullypolice.org

Rosalind Wiseman . . . . www.rosalindwiseman.com

Mythology by Edith Hamilton, Little, Brown and Company (1942).

Don't Know Much About Mythology by Kenneth C. Davis, HarperCollins (2005).

Wicca: A Guide for the Solitary Practitioner by Scott Cunningham, Llewellyn Publications (2004).

Wicca for Beginners: Fundamentals of Philosophy & Practice by Thea Sabin, Llewellyn Publications (2006).

Witches, Midwives & Nurses by Barbara Ehrenreich & Deirdre English, The Feminist Press (2010).

Woman as Healer, A Panoramic Survey of the Healing Activities of Women from Prehistoric Times to the Present by Jeanne Achterberg, Shambhala Publications, Inc. (1990).

A History of Witchcraft, Sorcerers, Heretics & Pagans by Jeffrey B. Russell & Brooks Alexander, Thames & Hudson Ltd, London (1980, 2007).

The Witches' Voice . . . . www.witchvox.com

ABOUT THE AUTHOR

Author Karen A. Stansbury practiced law in Connecticut for twenty-four years. After enduring twenty years of courtroom litigation she became certified in mediation, hoping for a more peaceful life. She began posting helpful articles on her website, encouraging clients to choose a less stressful path to problem solving. Writing novels using real cases was the next logical step. Now she does it full time.

When Karen isn't writing or traveling, she's painting watercolor landscapes, or riding, or kayaking, or biking, or rowing, or cooking, or gardening. She lives in Litchfield County, Connecticut.